D0966410

GROUNDWORK GUIDES

Series Editor
Jane Springer

GROUNDWORK GUIDES

Hip Hop World
Dalton Higgins

Groundwood Books
House of Anansi Press

Toronto Berkeley

Groundwood Books / House of Anansi Press
110 Spadina Avenue, Suite 801, Toronto, Ontario M5V 2K4
or c/o Publishers Group West
1700 Fourth Street, Berkeley, CA 94710

We acknowledge for their financial support of our publishing
program the Canada Council for the Arts, the Government of Canada
through the Book Publishing Industry Development Program (BPIDP)
and the Ontario Arts Council.

 ONTARIO ARTS COUNCIL
CONSEIL DES ARTS DE L'ONTARIO

Library and Archives Canada Cataloguing in Publication
Hip hop world / Dalton Higgins.
(Groundwork guides)
ISBN 978-0-88899-910-8 (bound).—ISBN 978-0-88899-911-5 (pbk.)
1. Hip-hop. I. Title. II. Series: Groundwork guides
ML3531.H636 2009   782.421'649   C2009-902744-5

Design by Michael Solomon
Printed and bound in Canada

Contents

Chapter 1
The Audacity of Hip Hop

I love the art of hip hop, I don't always love the message of hip hop...there is a message that is not only sometimes degrading to women, not only uses the N word a little too frequently, but also, something I'm really concerned about, is always talking about material things...The question is, imagine something different. Imagine communities that aren't torn up by violence. Imagine communities where we're respecting our women...where knowledge and reading and academic excellence are valued...Art can't just be a rear view mirror — it should have a headlight out there, according to where we need to go.

— Jay-Z fan, American president Barack Obama[1]

It's a hip hop world, and you're just living in it. For most music-addicted earthlings, hip hop culture is the predominant global youth subculture of today. For the non-music initiated, hip hop has become the black, jewelry-laden elephant in a room filled with rock, country and classical music — an attention-grabber whose influence is impossible to miss on the daily news, in school playgrounds, during water cooler conversations or in a political debate.

What is hip hop, and why should you care about it? Hip hop — a term coined by pioneering rapper Space Cowboy in the early 1970s to mimic a scat and then popularized later by rapper Lovebug Starski — is quite simply the world's leading counterculture, subculture and youth culture. Hip hop encompasses four distinct elements: deejaying (the manipulation of pre-recorded music), breakdancing (dance), rapping/emceeing (vocalizing) and graffiti (visual art).

For starters, curious onlookers have to acknowledge its success as a massive chart-topping, revenue-generating music movement. When rapper Jay-Z's (Shawn Carter) *American Gangster* disc opened on top of the pop charts in 2007, that gave him ten *Billboard* number one albums in ten years, tying him with the King of Rock, Elvis Presley, for the most chart-toppers by a solo artist.[2] Likewise, at a time when CD sales are plummeting, rapper Lil Wayne's *Tha Carter III* was the number one selling album of 2008 in the US, scanning an astounding three million units.

Much has been written about hip hop's gritty African American origins in the South Bronx, but the primary American consumers are young suburban whites whose fascination with black youth culture has led to Caucasian rappers Eminem and the Beastie Boys becoming creators of both the fastest selling rap album in history (*The Marshall Mathers LP*) and the first rap album to go number one on the *Billboard* album charts (*Licensed to Ill*), respectively. Once a predominantly African American youth form of expression, or as legendary hip hop group Public Enemy's lead vocalist Chuck D once called it, the "black people's CNN," rap has taken root around the world as a primary news source for disenfranchised Asian, South Asian, First Nations, Latin American, Australasian, African, Middle Eastern and European publics.

Forty-plus years after its birth, hip hop has officially grown up and left the 'hood. Hip hoppers own palatial estates in exclusive gated communities and are world travelers racking up Air Miles in abundance.[3]

From New York to Nigeria, hip hop is so wildly popular that it's crossing continents and oceans, and by many accounts its brightest future star might come in the form of an already wealthy, bi-racial (Jewish/black), Lil Wayne-tutored Canadian rapper named Drake. The incorporation, appropriation and wholesale celebration of the music has taken shape internationally, far from its American birthplace. Take Japan, where despite language barriers many Japanese youth have aped African American rappers' stylings by tanning their skin dark brown (*ganguro* or "blackface") and wearing cornrows and dreadlocks. In Cuba, former president Fidel Castro refers to rap music as the "vanguard of the Revolution." In Iran, heads of state complain that rap's obscene lyrics diminish Islamic values, and its influence is so pervasive that it has been officially banned. In France, it's considered the unofficial voice of the *banlieues* — the impoverished suburbs where African and Arab youth have staged violent anti-racism riots. Native American and aboriginal Canadian youth work out of the tradition of spoken-word iconoclast John Trudell, rapping out against past and present wrongdoings in their respective reserves and communities.

In North America, no comparable art form or music genre draws so many multiculti consumers to cash registers, music downloading websites and live concerts. Cultural critics point out that at rock'n'roll, classical or country music concerts, sometimes the only things that are "of color" are the stage curtains — and even them curtains ain't got no soul. Rap music, on the other hand, is anti-classical, a UN-friendly music with dozens upon dozens of subgenres to accommodate and account for the full range of experiences that make up the human condition — irrespective of one's race, gender, age or geography.

If you're gay or lesbian, there's a burgeoning Homo Hop movement. If you like your violence and sex gratuitous, there are large Gangsta Rap and Horrorcore Rap factions. If you're Jewish or a born-again Christian, the Klezmer or Christian Rap scenes might suit your fancy. And if you're a geek and rap music seems altogether too hipster and cool to comprehend, there's a large Nerdcore Rap movement where you and fellow squares can sink your cerebellums into raps about deoxyribonucleic acid patterns and nuclear physics.

Hip hop's adaptability becomes even more marked internationally because at its genesis rap music essentially involves creating something out of nothing. During the 1980s, Reaganomics wiped out inner-city school music funding programs in the US, leaving low-income youth to their own devices.[4] Manipulating vinyl records on turntables to make music replaced violin and horn sections, and spoken-word diatribes replaced organized vocal choir practices. Today, in a similar vein, Native American youth on reserves don't need to be classically trained in a musical instrument or attend a costly music conservatory to create rap music. And neither do youth in Africa, the poorest continent in the world, where the rap scene is blossoming at a faster pace than in any other region. Groups can simply utilize their lips, tongues and mouths to create the vocal percussion music — or "human beat box" sounds usually created by drum machine-produced beats — that forms the backbone of some of the best universal rap tracks of all time, like "La Di Da Di" by Doug E. Fresh.

But don't get it twisted. The world is not a greater place because of rap music. The genre is not a panacea for global famine, nor is it encouraging us to hold hands and sing "Kumbaya" with our multicultured brothers and sisters around the planet. Not even close. Rap music actually dominates headlines for being quite the opposite — an unrepentant outlaw music that magnifies the darker side of black.

Despite societal well-wishers hoping to see some sort of Obamaian racial progress shift taking place under the aegis of hip hop, when we look at real measurements of equality — access to education, housing, politics — we can see that it's just not happening fast enough. Sure, youth from around the world from all cultural backgrounds are downloading the same Young Jeezy songs as a collective global unit and fanbase. But the economic conditions between them aren't changing much. What exactly are privileged Western rap audiences — who are listening to the same rap music as say youth in Brazilian favelas — doing to eradicate extreme poverty in Rio? Isn't that what rap was intended to do — speak and act out against oppression — not just rhyme and dance to it?

This is the crafty nature of rap. It acts as a virtual magnet for controversy and scandal because rap music's vanguards spend much of their recording time replaying what the real issues are, including what dystopia looks, smells and feels like, with their words. It's a pure artistic response to oppression — protest music where art truly imitates life, its music intended to play back society's most celebratory and inflammatory aspects.

As politicians increasingly refuse to address genuine social inequalities, rappers speak about the beauty and ugliness of the world with equal candor, putting up a sharp mirror to reality. And they've received heavy verbal critiques for coming off so raw and uncut. Some of the genre's most cogent songs, for example, come in the form of blunt responses to police brutality in African American communities. They include anthems like "Fuck Tha Police," a searing indictment of racial profiling by the LAPD (Los Angeles Police Department) recorded by one of rap's most influential groups, N.W.A. (Niggaz With Attitude), and musically re-tooled by one of its greatest producers, the late J Dilla, to address Detroit area police all the way to Ice-T's "Cop Killer," which calls for frustrated victims of anti-black police misconduct to "dust some cops off" (shoot or stab crooked cops). Clearly, the rapperati have no intention of getting Rodney Kinged, and aren't afraid to tell you.

When the music is not taking vicious verbal swipes at injustices, it's doling out bushels of lyrics that carry some of the most offensive words in the English language. A mini-alphabet of forbidden words, including the B- and F-word, appear with nauseating frequency. These are words that don't get remote consideration for inclusion on the CDs of other music genres. And would the use of the explosive N-word be debated today on CNN, in bar-bershops or in strip malls around the world if not for hip hop? Rap is the only genre of music where the term is widely used, despite most of its leading figures being African American, the community for whom the word was created by racists to disparage. N-word debates have flared up frequently in the US over the last few years, from shock jocks Don Imus to Bounty Hunter Duane "Dog" Chapman to Seinfeld's Michael "Kramer" Richards — all non-black performers who've used the term, implicitly claiming they are taking the lead from hip hop. Critics have also long argued that rap music's sexually explicit lyrics — where the use of "bitch" and "ho" to describe women and the unrepentant use of the word "fag(got)" are commonplace — contribute to the moral breakdown of society.

Who's to blame for all of this? Who really profits from the cartoonish rap stereotypes of young black maledom that African Americans have been trying to shake for decades? Some argue that hip hop is simply a byproduct of a society that is equally foul-mouthed, sexist, racist and homophobic. Should the African American community be held accountable for the dissemination of such vile, lewd language and imagery? Or does the responsibility lie with the largely non-black recording label presidents of multimillion-dollar corporations who draft up and sign contracts with these musicians? Is there a reason many non-Western hip hop artists and critics have held their tongues in debates over the use of the N-word? Are black community broadcasters like BET (Black Entertainment Television) that traffic the negative elements of the culture to global audiences complicit? When BET rotates graphically sexist videos to audiences in Canada and the UK around the clock, are they aware of the global effects on their young female — and male — constituencies?

Once a form of social protest in the United States, rap appears to be anything but that now. Outside of the US, where rap music is articulating and addressing local political and social concerns, it presents a remarkable contrast. Tapping into hip hop's potential as a force for social change should be easy to realize, given that it boasts an active, captive, global youth base. But can we realistically expect solutions to complex world problems from teens and twenty-something rappers? More importantly, is hip hop immune from the same historical processes that turned historically black musics like jazz and rock'n'roll into pale shades of their former selves, genres enjoyed, profited from and largely consisting of performers from every other ethnic group but that of the creators?

As for the future of rap, are performers still able to sing the blues, or authentically rap about the 'hood, when some of the conditions that created rap have changed? Or since its vanguards such as so-called "gangsta" rappers Ice Cube and Snoop Dogg have become multimillionaires? Before we can penetrate these debates and project where hip hop is going, we have to understand where hip hop music culture came from in the first place, where it is now and how it works.

Chapter 2
The Old School and the Elements

Hip hop has clearly left its mark on global contemporary music, art, politics, culture and fashion. But in the beginning, no one imagined that a music form dismissed in the US as an urban youth fad would be so widely accepted around the globe.

What we now refer to as hip hop has its roots in decaying 1970s South Bronx neighborhoods where unemployment rates among young blacks and Latinos were sky-high, running between 60 and 80 percent.[1] Out of this concrete jungle emerged a symbolic rose by the name of DJ Kool Herc. Born in Kingston, Jamaica, Herc emigrated to New York in 1967, introducing the Jamaican sound system deejay-led party rituals to American music culture. By hosting huge street parties, presciently including talented female rhymers like Pebblee Poo to accompany his sound system in an intrinsically male-dominated subculture, and spinning music on two sets of turntables at gatherings in unconventional places like the recreation room of an apartment building at 1520 Sedgwick Avenue, Herc was able to engage bitter street gang rivals on — of all places — the dance floor. As the lone supplier of music to dance to, the deejay became the first key element in early hip hop culture. And it was Herc's innovative manipulation of the vinyl records that made these occasions something special.

Re-playing different elements of two records that were spinning at the same time to extend the songs, Herc would then find the "break" beat — the part of the song where a singer takes a break and the instrumental takes over — so that he could excite and acknowledge the party's guests. He could do this without competing with the pre-recorded vocals on the record he was spinning. This technique had long been a part of the Jamaican "toasting" ritual, which features a vocalist improvising or chanting rehearsed words over the "riddim" (rhythm), the instrumental part of the record. These break beats provided the foundation for the break boys or b-boy crews, the dancers who performed on the dance floor during these breaks. Many of the dancers were gang-affiliated youth who chose to "battle" on the dance floor rather than on street corners.

Pioneers like Afrika Bambaataa and his Zulu Nation, made up of former gang members, were dedicated to teaching youth self-pride and cultural awareness through music and dance. Bambaataa had a huge record collection of funk, disco, African and Latin music, and he threw massive parties that provided a haven for youth of all cultures to dance together. Under the tutelage of the Zulu Nation, they settled their beefs on the dance floor and breakdancing became another key element in hip hop's origins. Bambaataa's prescient vision for hip hop's global breakout shows up later, in his Bronx-shaped breakdance anthem "Planet Rock," which took its inspiration from the groundbreaking German electronic band Kraftwerk, whose "Trans-Europe Express" melody he re-used in the song.

While breakdancing has African roots in martial arts like the Brazilian Capoeira, different styles and crews emerged in New York and Los Angeles in the 1970s. The Latin American and, more specifically, Puerto Rican influence and retentions in the creation of hip hop's early dance moves was undeniable, but remains underreported.[2] Many of the pioneering b-boy crews like Rock Steady Crew and New York City Breakers were heavily populated with Puerto Rican youth who intermingled with Caribbean immigrants and African Americans in the South Bronx. The Puerto Ricans adopted Cuban mambo-infused dance styles, influencing the "floor work" breakdance staples you see in modern hip hop routines. The Bronx-based Rock Steady Crew innovated the "uprock" dance form of movement that has dancers engaging in a rhythmic "fight" without contact. "Locking," the robotic body movements started by Lockatron Jon and Shabba-Doo in Los Angeles, captured the consciousness of urban youth.

The whole idea of what we now consider rap — rhyming lyrics chanted to musical accompaniment — originated in West Africa, where oral historians called griots carried this unique ability to weigh in on current events, provide comic relief and tell stories while playing the djembe (a goblet-shaped wooden hand drum covered with goatskin).[3]

In the US, pre-rap music inspiration comes from the Last Poets, composed of lyricists Abiodun Oyewole, Umar Bin Hassan, Alafia Pudim and drum player Nilaja, who got together in New York during the American civil rights era (they formed on Malcolm X's forty-third birthday, May 19, 1968). Their street poetry, fusing spoken-word diatribes with singing and chanting, delivered messages about African Americans' self-awareness.

Viewed by many as the "godfather of rap," Gil Scott-Heron performed a rare combination of soul, funk and wordplay during the 1970s. Heron's debut *Small Talk at 125th and Lenox* album included "The Revolution Will Not Be Televised," a criticism of the media, and one of this militant activist's best-known songs.

Working out of this ages-old tradition of storytelling in African villages, hip hop's first recognized rappers appeared in the mid-1970s. Coke La Rock, hip hop's first acknowledged emcee by virtue of being the first to rap along to Herc's deejay set music, and then hip hop's first Latino emcee, Prince Whipper Whip, made up crafty improvised rhymes and engaged in impressive call-and-response routines with audiences.

Around the same time, the New York City subway system became a line of communication between warring youth from all five boroughs (Queens, the Bronx, Manhattan, Brooklyn and Long Island). Philadelphia writers Cornbread and Kool Earl had kicked off the modern-day graffiti movement in the 1960s. Later, crews in New York were figuring out that they could leave their mark on their territory and the wider city by scribbling their names on surfaces in subways or train yards with markers, pens and spray paint. Graffiti artists would ride the subway "tagging" (writing their signature on) as many subway cars as possible, and soon realized that they could tag many more subway cars in train yards without bombing (getting caught).

Tagging began in New York City in the early 1970s with Vic, a mail courier who rode the local subways and buses to deliver his packages. He allegedly set a goal for himself to visit every subway and ride every bus in NYC and began to write his name and courier ID number (156) on each one. And when a young Greek delivery messenger named Demetrius began writing "Taki 183" all over the city, he so popularized the craft that many young hip hoppers followed his lead and turned blank walls into their own unauthorized canvases.

All of hip hop's four core elements – deejaying, break-dancing, rapping/emceeing and graffiti – have their own unique languages and skill sets. For example, under the deejay umbrella lies the skill of turntablism, which involves manipulating vinyl records on turntables to create new sounds.

Hip hop enjoyed its first breakthrough gold-selling hit single in 1979 with "Rapper's Delight." By the time the seminal song came out, with the rhymes, "I said a hip hop, a hippie a hippie, to the hip hip hop, you don't stop a rockin', to the bang bang boogy, say up jump the boogy, to the rhythm of the boogity beat," the other tenets of the culture had already taken flight.

Jamaican Roots

What Mecca is to Muslims, New York is to rap—hip hop Holy Land, with Los Angeles or Atlanta being rap's Medina. Despite what many Western rap critics and historians think and write, Jamaica should be added to this list of rap birthplaces, forming a Holy Trinity of landmark locales for rap to call home.

The Caribbean region in general supplied hip hop with its first rapper, Jamaican-born Coke La Rock, and its three main legendary deejays, from Barbados-born Grandmaster Flash, who invented the "turntablism" concept before it had a name, to Afrika Bambaataa, the "godfather of hip hop" who's of Barbadian and Jamaican lineage, to hip hop's founding father, Jamaican-born DJ Kool Herc, the culture's first acknowledged deejay. Without Herc there is no hip hop. Besides rap's founding father being Jamaican-born and bred, the rapper most often cited by fans and critics alike to be the greatest of all time, the Notorious B.I.G., also "grew up in Jamaica," spending every summer of his first sixteen years going "back home" to Trelawny and hanging out with his extended family, including his disc jockey uncle Dave who played at local area reggae clubs.[4]

However, the Jamaican reggae influence and retentions in hip hop go much deeper. Rap and reggae, as art forms that carry tremendous global cultural impact, share many similarities. Both are byproducts of black ghetto life responding to the socio-economic conditions of exclusion, poverty, race and class oppression. In addition, Jamaican deejay U-Roy's pre-hip hop toasting rhyme style pre-dates what is known as rapping in America by over a decade.

The list of celebrated rappers who claim Jamaica is wide and varied, and includes rap's most versatile voice, Busta Rhymes; Heavy D, one of rap's first plus-size stars, who punctuated his rhymes with patois-infused scats ("bad didlee didlee dee"); Chubb Rock, whose "Treat Em Right" was in 2008 voted the eighty-second best song in VH1's 100 Greatest Songs of Hip Hop; Canadian hip hop ambassador Kardinal Offishall, whose distinct dancehall-rap fusion sound landed him on *Billboard* chart-topping solo artist Akon's Kon Live label; Pete Rock, considered one of the greatest hip hop producers of all time; and M1 (Dead Prez), one of the most respected politico rappers in the world.

The history of Jamaican settlement in the US can be traced to the passing of the US 1965 Immigration Act. By the 1980s, 9 percent of Jamaica's population of 2.5 million people were in the US, with almost half of them living in New York.[5] Jamaican music went in and out of vogue over the next few decades. Jamaican reggae king Bob Marley burst out on global pop charts in the 1970s with his *Catch a Fire* debut, and subsequently his 1984 *Legend* release became the best-selling reggae album of all time. In 2001, Shaggy's *Hot Shot* was the number one album in the US, selling over six million copies in that country alone.

But during the 1960s in New York, reggae was still considered "jungle music." In fact, Herc as an immigrant youth in NYC spent a lot of time unlearning his Jamaican accent in order to fit in.[6] And while much has been written about how he transported Jamaican deejay culture to the South Bronx, the break records he became popular for spinning weren't reggae tunes but funk ones from American funksters like James Brown.

The overwhelming influence of a migrated Jamaican music product and performance style on rap music became evident on KRS-One's *Criminal Minded* (1987). KRS-One uses considerable mic time on the reggae-influenced rap hit "The Bridge Is Over" to diss rival MC Shan over where he thinks rap's American roots lie. It's an exchange of recorded insults that Jamaican DJ's Prince Jazzbo and I Roy engaged in ten years earlier. "The Bridge Is Over" set the early qualitative standard for American rap diss records, with both artists recording a series of songs back and forth to lay claim to the true geographical birthplace borough of hip hop — South Bronx vs. Queensbridge (Queens).

The widespread adoption of Jamaican music and culture became all the more clear by the early 1990s when a whole slew of rappers who weren't of Jamaican descent began to rhyme in patois or "nation language" and wear Rastafarian dreadlocks hairstyles. New York-based bands ranged from the Fu-Schnickens (lead rapper Chip Fu is of Trinidadian and Barbados parentage), whose dance-hall-influenced "Ring the Alarm" samples reggae staple Wayne Smith's "Ring the Alarm"; to Das EFX, who wore dreadlocks; to groups like Black Moon, Smif-N-Wessun and Mos Def, who used patois in their rhymes. Even rap's first megastar band, Run DMC, demonstrated a Jamaican musical influence in "Roots, Rap, Reggae," featuring Yellowman, although it came off sounding inauthentic and trite. Bad reggae, even worse rap.

With the 1990s invention and explosion of dancehall music, an offshoot of reggae, rap's closest global music cousin is even more clearly defined. Dancehall performers operate like emcees rapping or "chatting," as opposed to roots reggae artists who sing over various largely instrumental rhythms that can stand on their own as songs. The rhythmic rhyming of vocals in Jamaican dancehall is not only nearly identical to the development of rapping in African American hip hop, but the battle or "clash" element, which pits rival rhymers against each other to see who's best, shares the same function. Also, dancehall, like rap, has its own large and clearly defined witty insider slanguage. A dancehall artist might say *bandulu*, which means engaging in criminal activity, or call a party a *bashment*.

A slew of dancehall-rap fusions aiming to unite the two related traditions were performed by dancehall artists toasting over hip hop beats — Capleton and Q-Tip's "Original Man," Shabba Ranks and Chubb Rock's "Two Breddrens" — but were met with disinterest in the American marketplace. Despite these setbacks, rap icon Nas has teamed up with Damian Marley (reggae legend Bob's youngest son) in a gutsy effort to link the two musical traditions with their *Distant Relatives* release.

Other artists like Junior Reid, Bounty Killer, Buju Banton and Super Cat are embraced by hip hop constituencies around the globe for their ability to chat over dancehall or rap instrumental rhythms with equal efficiency.

People who think that rap is dead or that the genuine angst once felt in rap is largely gone argue that reggae and dancehall are more genuine rebel musics for these times because the conditions that created them are still there: poverty, unemployment, class warfare. Unlike multimillionaire rappers such as 50 Cent or T.I. (Clifford Joseph Harris Jr.), who collude with multinational companies to market and brand themselves, the largely Rastafarian-based A-list reggae performers like Sizzla or Capleton, who dominate the dancehall charts, spend considerable recording time speaking out against what they view as an oppressive system (dubbed Shitstem) and scold Babylon (which can be interpreted as police or government). It's the reason why many hip hop fans are infatuated with dancehall — it's pure unfiltered outlaw music, like rap once was. It's about time everyone "bigs up" (gives respect) to the vital contributions of the many Jamaican-descended hip hoppers who paved the way for its global penetration and continue to influence the shaping of the music.

Human Beat Box
Human beat boxers sit alongside car salespeople and telemarketers as bottom feeders in the fragile employment social order. Their throats are deep, and their influence on global hip hop is huge.

To the hip hop uninitiated, it may appear odd to see a whole youth subculture cupping their hands around their lips, trying to make belching and burping noises sound funky. But it's impossible not to be amazed when you are walking down a city street or rural area and hear the boom bap beats of James Brown's "Funky Drummer" coming from a drum kit. Except that there is no drum is considered by many cultural critics to be the first pre-rap song because he talks in rhymes, much like a modern-day rapper.

Rudy Ray Moore AKA Dolemite — Dolemite is a widely known American singer and comedian made famous as the "king of party records" for his trash-talking abilities first seen in his role as a pimp in the 1975 movie *Dolemite*. His deft comedy routines were spoken in the same toasting rhyming style that rappers now employ.

James Brown — Without James Brown, the late "godfather of soul," there would be no hip hop. His "Funky Drummer" song is considered to be the most "sampled" record in history and a major building block for hip hop. (Sampling is taking a snippet of an audio recording and repro-cessing it for use another way, on another song. See page 42.) In the 1960s, before the term "rap" was coined, Brown released songs of social uplift like "America Is My Home," whose vocal delivery sounds like early rap.

Dub Poetry — Dub is a Jamaican-birthed spoken-word form that is per-formed over reggae rhythms. This form of performance poetry developed in the 1970s around the same time as rap's voice was developing under the tutelage of another seminal Jamaican figure, DJ Kool Herc. Genre innovators Linton Kwesi Johnson and Oku Onuora released seminal recordings *Dread Beat an' Blood* and *Reflections in Red*, respectively.

kit. Just a kid named Muhammad and another named Ezra standing there. And they *are* the drum kit — mim-icking those funky sounds, minus the snares, cymbals, toms or even drumsticks.

Beat boxing is a style of vocal percussion initiated to form a musical backdrop to rap performances, but that is now a musical act on its own. While it began as an

American phenomenon, it has since taken off around the world, and it's no surprise. After all, musicians from around the globe have always been using their tongues to make clicking sounds (clicks are a part of the language of the South African Saan); their throats to make other-worldly, awesome gurgling and singing sounds (e.g., Tuvan and Inuit throat singing); and their lips to make purring musical sounds (e.g., China's kouji) or to simulate the sounds of a live orchestra or band (see Killa Kela Sounds Off, pages 30-31).

While the wider hip hop culture's main elements are now getting highbrow recognition — in 2006, the Smithsonian National Museum of American History agreed to house a permanent collection of hip hop artifacts — beat boxing has always been treated like hip hop's redheaded stepchild, an acknowledged part of the hip hop family, but an oddity. It's been called hip hop's Fifth Element.[7]

While you can find many rap, breakdance, graffiti and deejay practitioners making a decent living from their craft, you would be hard-pressed to find many people with the beat boxer job title who don't have to do other jobs to make ends meet. The peculiar thing about their presence on the rap landscape is that they often play the role of hip hop's lifeguard, applying first aid when equipment meltdowns happen and rappers need backing music. Beat boxers often come on stage to save the day, replaying back sounds that a laptop music program might have created or that a live band was supposed to have played before the "technical difficulties."

Beat boxers are the eccentrics of hip hop, highly visible but massively misunderstood. How else can you explain the fact that many of them idolize middling 1980s actor Michael Winslow from those Police Academy films? They view him as a messiah for his ability to create otherworldly sounds on a dime.

American Barry B. created the term "beat box" in the early 1980s to describe the incredible rhythms being generated by his musically inclined peer Doug E. Fresh and other inner-city artists who mastered the art of imitating early drum-machine sounds with their vocal cords, at times sounding even more musical than the recordings themselves.

One could argue that a competent beat box performance or improvisation is similar to scatting in American jazz, where vocalists improvise instrumental melodies like musical instruments. It can also be compared to *puirt a beul*, a style of mouth music indigenous to Cape Breton, Scotland and Ireland, which is used to replicate the sound of a bagpipe or fiddle and is so rhythmic that it overshadows the actual words being said.

The first real rap-specific mouth music form emerged in New York in the 1980s with the late Darren "Buffy" Robinson (Fat Boys) and soloist Doug E. Fresh who applied these skills and sounds to vinyl on "Human Beat Box" and "Pass the Buddha," respectively.

The emergence of beat boxing falls in line with hip hop culture's other elements — inventing a music practice out of nothing. Buying recording equipment wasn't easy for Latin American and African American households in

Killa Kela Sounds Off

Killa Kela, a white guy from West Sussex, England, is the world's greatest beat boxer, next to The Roots' Rahzel, "The Godfather of Noise," from Philadelphia. In an online interview with me in 2008, Kela shared his secrets of how he uses his various body parts to create new musical compositions and remix older ones.

How did you learn this beat box skill?

I remember being seven or eight and copying my dad playing the drums on his practice tapes. Then came TV soundtracks, where I'd put beats over television theme songs and cartoons. It wasn't really serious at that age at all. I just thought it was normal and an expressive part of growing up. It was only when I was twelve years old that I heard an old mix tape with Biz Markie performing live at Brixton Academy in London. He was beat boxing and when I heard it, aside from all the other hip hop elements I knew about, this was my entrance to something I really felt I could be good at. It felt exclusive, special, for an elite few that really knew how to do it. So I got down and decided to create my own snares and sounds.

But it was only when I heard Rahzel (I think I was fifteen) that I realized what I was doing was right. I had been practicing and creating sounds based off influences such as the Prodigy, Stereo MCs, Jungle Music and a lot of modern-day hip hop. When Rahzel came on the scene, he redefined what beat boxers were doing in the American spotlight and, in turn, all around the world. It was only a matter of time before the UK would look for a British equivalent — so I got to work.

Reagan-era New York, so some enterprising youth started crafting their own sounds with their mouths to mimic the sounds of the beat-making machines they couldn't afford. It didn't require any plug-ins, power outlets or storage cases. It was as low tech as it gets. The only pre-

Eighteen was when I first got on stage. By twenty I had done two world tours and was a member of the Scratch Perverts and the UK Rock Steady Crew.

Do you need any formal vocal training so you don't strain your vocal cords?

I think I may have done two or three vocal lessons when I had my first (record) deal. It was great because it taught me all about singing, which in turn benefited my beat boxing completely. Straining is always a worry, but beat boxing (I've found) isn't like singing. You're not gonna damage your voice with the kind of minimal sounds you're doing with such small projection. Also, I work with the microphone as an additional instrument to my voice — always have. So generally speaking, my voice doesn't take the flack or strain like that. Yo, mic control is an art in itself!

Are human beat boxers treated as real musicians or as a novelty act by fellow musicians?

Hmmm, I think it all depends on who you are and if you have a name. I say that because it takes a lot to shrug off that perception — "just a beat boxer." The biggest culprits are emcees. They'll rap all over you at a show for the novelty factor, they barely credit you or say your name, then the audience go home calling you "that" beat boxer. It took me ages to develop my name and be taken seriously as a musician for that very reason. Nowadays, I'm playing with every instrument and artist imaginable. And a lot of times, it's the "real" musicians (drummers, string players, producers, songwriters) that have embraced me most out of everyone in my career.

requisites to practice or play the human beat box are clear vocal cords and some will — unless you're nursing a cold or flu.

While African Americans like Buffy Robinson of the Fat Boys and Doug E. Fresh became innovators by crafting these sounds and actually making them sound funky and danceable (it's one thing to create guttural sounds as a novelty, another thing to make them sound like dance floor-friendly music), it's actually outside of the US that the ripple effect of this genius art form is being felt. Kenny Muhammad or Rahzel from The Roots, hip hop's most respected live band, are now the torchbearers. European youth in particular have been lapping up the beat box skills and spirit since the 1990s, when beat boxing seemed to be getting pushed to the music underground scene.

Three of the four international beat box conventions were held outside the US. Boxcon (the International Human Beatbox Convention), which started in 2003, is held annually in London, England. The first world championship of beat boxing took place in Germany and was won by an Australian, Joel Turner. In England, another world champ, Killa Kela, incorporates performance-art elements and body movements into the usual repertoire of replaying popular songs and vocal scratching (imitating sounds of a turntable scratching).

Breakdancing Boyz and Girlz

Just the mere thought of spinning on your back twenty-five consecutive times might make your head spin. But it's just another day at the office for the typical break boy or girl. It's simple. You take a piece of cardboard from an old furniture delivery box and dance like nobody's watching. You are connecting yourself to a worldwide community of dancers whose palette is a piece of cardboard or slab of linoleum placed on a floor.

Word of Mouth

There are a number of uniquely talented beat box-esque mouth musicians around the globe who aren't hip hop practitioners, but who produce sophisticated musical sounds with their lips, tongues and throats, among other body parts — the vocal percussion skill is not specific to hip hop.

Björk (Iceland): Her 2004 album *Medúlla* is constructed almost entirely of human vocals, with global human beat boxers like Japan's Dokaka, the UK's Shlomo and Philadelphia's Rahzel foremost among them.

Vocal Sampling (Cuba): This Grammy-nominated six-member all-male a cappella ensemble reproduce with their vocal cords all of the sounds of the instruments in a typical Latin orchestra, including horns and percussion.

Tanya Tagaq (Canada): This Inuit throat singer's avant garde vocal grunts, gasps and groans imitate the sounds of nature and wildlife, and are linked to her Inuit culture's throat-singing traditions. In Inuit tradition, for entertainment two women from a tribe face each other and go back and forth producing complementary vocal rhythmic sounds.

T. H. Subash Chandran (India): Chandran performs Carnatic, a South Asian classical music that displays a remarkable optimizing of vocal cord performance. Interestingly, human beat boxing is thought to carry some ages-old Indian bol music retentions (bol forms a crucial component of South Asian rhythm sections).

Bobby McFerrin (US): This Grammy-winning jazz and classical musician is best known for hit song "Don't Worry, Be Happy" and his vocal explorations that sometimes connect Tuvan throat-singing practices (Tuva is in southern Siberia, close to Mongolia) with vocal percussion effects, chest taps and chanting. Interestingly, rap politico super group Public Enemy reference "Don't Worry" in their protest anthem "Fight the Power," slyly attacking its light, apolitical approach to daily living.

B-boying entered the public consciousness in the 1980s in North America when Hollywood began churning out blackbuster films like *Beat Street* and *Breakin'* (Parts I and II). Like anything else viewed as a fad, the overexposure crippled breakdancing's ability to be taken seriously as the lucid art form it was. As media attention faded, it went back underground in the US and got re-birthed outside of the country.

In Europe, South America and Asia, breakdancing never died or took a backseat to rapping. By the early 1990s, the dance scene was regenerated throughout Europe, where the largest competitions were originated, developed and staged. Battle of the Year and B-Boy Summit grew to become the central meeting place for spinning heads to "battle."

The annual Battle of the Year competition, started in 1990, is the oldest and largest gathering of dancers, with elimination rounds taking place in twenty-three different countries, generating audiences of sixty thousand. There is no global rap competition equivalent.

The non-North American practitioners evolved the form by adding a lot more artistry, theater and athleticism to what was an already dynamic dance form. For example, dance crews from Japan and Korea are credited with adding athleticism to staple dance moves like windmills (an acrobatic power move that involves twirling on the floor) and headspins (spinning on one's head while maintaining poise). A Korean or Japanese crew has won every Battle of the Year since 2000.[8] One member of South Korea's legendary Drifterz Crew, three-time UK B-

Boy Championship winners, says that Koreans tend to dominate the dance form because they "practice like it's a science. They break it down and study the parts," rehearsing for up to six hours a day.

Bruce Lee, B-Boy?

A large chunk of the traditional foundation breakdance moves believed to have been birthed in New York — including uprock (dancing upright along to the rhythm), windmills and headspins — carry the kung fu influence. Kung fu films, especially those starring Bruce Lee, were popular around the world during the mid to late 1970s. For example, windmills originated from a kung fu move that practitioners used to get up from the floor after a battle. Crazy Legs of the Rock Steady Crew incorporated this concept into his "dead man freeze" move. He then decided to make it continuous by repeating the move — and windmills were born.[9]

Was Bruce Lee an original b-boy? Not exactly. But in real life he was a Latin dancer, crowned the Hong Kong Crown Colony Cha-Cha champion in 1958.[10] And in his movies, he does a form of footwork that is very similar to what hip hoppers call "top rocking." If you dig in the DVD vaults and take a closer look at *Drunken Master* or *Shaolin Temple*, you'll see moves where an actor spins on his head 180 degrees or makes a whole rotation — which helped to make headspins a part of the b-boys' repertoire.

Verina Glaser writes in *Kung-Fu: Cinema of Vengeance* that "the basis for the success of the kung-fu films in the States was the same ghetto audience that carried the wave of 'black' Hollywood action films a year or so previously."[11] Why the connection between these two disparate cultures? Both New York and Hong Kong had high crime rates and rough ghettos. Kung fu films were escapist fantasies for the people of Hong Kong and they ended up serving the same purpose for American inner-city youth.

Even outside the realm of hip hop dance, rap giants Wu-Tang Clan appropriated the folklore and philosophy of kung fu movies, translating them into a multimillion-dollar hip hop empire. Their debut, *Enter the Wu-Tang (36 Chambers)*, is littered with references to Chinese hand-combat arts.

Spin Doctors

Turntables and CDJs (a CD player that functions like a turntable) have replaced guitars as the instrument of choice for alienated youth. And turntablism is a unique hip hop element practiced by Generation Next-ers that involves creating music and sounds with the use of turntables and a deejay mixer.

Turntablism was coined in 1994 to distinguish between deejays, who simply spin records, and actual turntable musicians, who use decks as instruments to sculpt and manipulate sounds. Much like a guitarist, drummer or bassist, turntablists have been lobbying to be recognized as genuine musicians who can produce tour-worthy music.

Two Technics 1200 turntables plugged into a Vestax mixer, used with Serato Scratch Live, is the art form's

Holy Grail, and it takes extreme amounts of hand-eye coordination and dexterity to pull off the tricks of this trade. Although not dubbed turntablism, back spin effects date back as far as 1968 on Creedence Clearwater Revival's self-titled debut where the trick is utilized on "Walk On the Water." In the early 1900s, experimental composers such as John Cage sampled and created music on his "Imaginary Landscape No. 1" (1939) using only his turntable.[12]

Pinoy Power

Rap historians and fans have always wondered why certain communities gravitate more toward hip hop culture than others and how they come to dominate one of the elements of the culture. When Edison invented the modern turntable over a century ago, he could never have imagined that it would be utilized as a musical instrument in its own right by enterprising Filipino youth.

There is a justifiably large amount of attention paid to Grand Wizard Theodore, who in 1976 accidentally invented scratching after bumping into his turntables while avoiding his mother's pleas to turn down the volume. He then recreated the sounds for artistic purposes. But not nearly enough respect is given to Luis "DJ Disco Wiz" Cedeno, hip hop culture's first Latino deejay. In 1977, he invented the "mixed plate" technique of merging sound bites with special effects and paused beats. And what about Grandmaster Flash, who took this one step further in the 1980s, using turntable manipulations to create sounds that mimic a live band? The all-Filipino deejay crew Invisibl Skratch Piklz took these skill sets to a whole new level.

Would hip hop culture have grown as it did without the Filipinos' crucial contributions? Absolutely not. And why do this community's hip hop scenesters gravitate toward turntablism, and not rapping or graffiti? Is it because, as Filipino DJs Rhettmatic and Babu suggest half-jokingly, after the "many years of using chopsticks, our dexterity is perfect for DJ'ing"?[13]

In a 2008 interview with me, Toronto-based former World 2003 DMC (Disco Mix Club) champion, and now MTV Live (Canada) resident deejay, DJ Dopey, who is Filipino, admits: "It always did baffle me how many Filipinos were in the scene. Not only doing it, but somewhat ruling it. I mean, you can always argue the power of numbers type thing, but it's definitely more than just that. I think with so many Filipinos in the scene, crews formed left, right and center. With this came internal competition and motivation within the crews that just kept everybody fresh and on top of their games. With regards to role models coming up, I had plenty from Qbert and the rest of the Piklz tearing up the West coast."

Filipino DJ Qbert, a co-founding member of Invisibl Skratch Piklz, often cited as the most prolific turntablist of this era, told me in an online interview in 2009 that Filipinos have a long tradition of musical entertaining, and turntablism is just a modern-day extension of it. "If you look at all the Pacific countries, you will find many

, entertainers that are Filipino," he says. "Probably because Filipinos come from a Third World country and art is all they have in many cases."

In hip hop, there is a democratizing function which sees to it that anyone with genuine skills supersedes any racial or cultural ownership of a single skill. That's why world hip hop turntablism competitions have Jewish-Canadian champs like A-Trak all the way to Filipino ones like DJ Qbert. There's no real gatekeeping function attached to mastering this skill set, unlike opera musicianship, which requires a certain degree of class or economic status to develop the skills.

The Invisibl Skratch Piklz, a pioneering California-based DJ crew composed of Filipino scratch masters Qbert, Shortkut, Mixmaster Mike and Apollo, have won nearly every deejay-mixing title, from the ITF (International Turntablist Federation) to the all-important world DMC championships. According to urban legend they were politely forced to retire by event organizers because their dominance stagnated the interest among up-and-coming deejays who knew they didn't stand a chance.[14]

The Filipino domination also shifted the singular focus away from New York and kicked open the door for other Filipino deejay crews like the Beat Junkies. This Filipino influence has extended its way to any city with a sizable *balikbayan* (overseas Filipino settlement). For example, there have been many top-ranked turntablist champions of Filipino descent from Canada, including 1998 World DMC and 1999 ITF World Beatjuggling

Champion Lil' Jaz (pop star Nelly Furtado's ex-boyfriend and father of her daughter, Nevis).

The Philippines boasts the oldest rap scene in southeast Asia, perhaps due to its historical relationship with the US.[15] It's also along the US West Coast, largely Los Angeles, and San Francisco's Bay Area, that you see a dynamic blend of the communities that birthed the genre, much as Puerto Rican settlements on the East Coast blended with that of African American cultures.

During the 1920s, working-class blacks, Filipinos and Mexicans partied together in taxi dancehalls — precursors of the LA nightclub scene and a byproduct of shared segregation into the neighborhoods of East and South Central Los Angeles.[16] Thousands more Filipino immigrants ended up in California during World War II to help fill the wartime labor shortage. Large numbers of Filipinos also migrated to the US during the 1970s, transforming San Francisco's Bay Area into the largest Filipino community outside of Manila (more than 50 percent of the population is Asian, with Chinese, followed by Filipinos, being the largest ethnic groups).[17]

From the late 1970s to the early 1990s, many, including DJ Qbert, began as mobile deejays at Filipino house parties, family gatherings and weddings. By 1987 there were over one hundred mobile deejay crews in the Bay Area.[18] It's these earlier settlers' children who initiated one of the greatest art forms of the twenty-first century — turntablism.

Today, many international touring rock and pop bands carry with them a deejay with turntablist skill sets to provide a sonic backdrop of sounds. Hardcore turntablists have taken that one step further. Not content to simply accompany bands as another instrument, they have formed full-on bands, where instead of having guitars, keyboards or drum kits, they mount a bunch of turntables to create sounds that can mimic or outperform a basic band setup. For example, France's Birdy Nam Nam and Montreal's Microtone Kitchen have perfected this, relying completely on a set of turntables as actual instruments to form a full band.

The future of turntablism will certainly involve a meshing of visuals with audio turntable scratches to create a full-on sensory overload. Explains DJ Dopey: "I didn't really go full force until Serato implemented a video plug-in. With video fully integrated, now I can still use my turntables and Serato vinyl to manipulate visuals along with the turntablism. It adds a new element to things and can potentially be much bigger than just the two turntables and a mixer routine."

But does the increased use of CDJs and other high-tech options mean the death of the two-turntables-and-vinyl format, an integral aspect of hip hop culture? Qbert doesn't think so. "That's like saying, 'does the invention of the keyboard mean the death of the grand piano?' Vinyl will never die because it has the highest accuracy when it comes to real hardcore scratching. But don't get me wrong, I love to use digital in my home studio to experiment. But intricate solos and the feel for subtleties just won't happen in a digital scratch. Ask any hardcore scratcher."

Sampling

Despite popular perceptions, sampling did not begin with hip hop. During the 1960s, pop bands like the Beach Boys used large elements of music from Chuck Berry's "Sweet Little Sixteen" to form their own hits like "Surfin' USA." Hip hoppers simply took the art of sampling to another creative level. By using inexpensive digital technology they borrowed fragments of old R&B records and re-tooled them by combining these sounds with modern ones. There are as many different ways to digitally reproduce, let's say, the sound of a horn section, drums or vocals as there are schools of thought on the skill involved. To some, sampling is a way of paying homage to legendary music masters who might otherwise have been forgotten. In 1979, the Sugar Hill Gang rapped over the entire "Good Times" instrumental by Chic to form hip hop's first big single "Rapper's Delight." To others, it looks like theft or appropriation by artists who lack the creativity to generate original compositions.

In the 1980s, James Brown instrumentals and vocals were sampled by dozens of artists to produce hits like Boogie Down Productions' "South Bronx" and Eric B & Rakim's "I Know You Got Soul." Run DMC further popularized the concept by sampling elements of non-urban rock music like Aerosmith's "Walk This Way," generating a big crossover hit. Still others like Diddy have built a career out of paying large sums of money to record companies who own the original music for the right to turn old hits by Diana Ross, David Bowie, Duran Duran or the Police (e.g., the Notorious B.I.G. tribute "I'll Be

Missing You" uses music from "Every Breath You Take") into chart-topping rap hits.

The other school of sampling holds that it takes even greater skill to manipulate original music into something beyond recognition. You shouldn't have to pay bloated multinational record companies who own the rights of original recordings to use portions of an original song when you've digitally made it unrecognizable. There is much controversy regarding artists sampling copyrighted material. Many musicians get legal permission to sample others' work, but it's gotten very costly.

A couple of big lawsuits in the late 1980s and early 1990s changed the way hip hoppers viewed unauthorized sampling forever.[19] The 1960s pop group the Turtles sued De La Soul and won, for using an unauthorized sample of their music on their *3 Feet High and Rising* album. Likewise, in 1991, Biz Markie's sampling of portions of a popular Gilbert O'Sullivan song was costly to his career, as it was ruled to be copyright infringement. When Bridgeport Music filed a lawsuit against eight hundred artists for using unauthorized snippets of George Clinton songs in 2001, a sampling chill effect took root in much of modern-day hip hop, robbing hip hop beat-makers and the genre itself of one of its most reliable and articulate staples — sample-based production. With the average cost to clear a sample sitting at $10,000[20] and the constant threat of lawsuits, many producers have forsaken the sample-based sound in favor of electronic-based production tools like synthesizers and Auto-Tune. They are also using a lot more live instrumentation or interpolation (musicians essentially replaying a sample with live musicians) because sampling fees have skyrocketed.

Then you have the case of Pittsburgh-based electronic recording artist Gregg "Girl Talk" Gillis. Gillis' 2008 album *Feed the Animals*, released on his aptly titled Illegal Art imprint, features more than three hundred easily recognizable uncleared samples, opening the gateway for a global discussion on who gets policed on copyright infringement and why. One would think that any musician who creates songs entirely made up of uncleared stitched-together samples might have stacks of lawsuits piling up, but he doesn't. Gillis seems to have found a legal loophole to keep the suits at bay, citing the "fair use" provision of copyright law. His argument is that he's creating new works by using the samples in unconventional ways. For example, a typical Girl Talk song might mash up popular pop, rap, reggae, country, folk and electronic music songs, all without missing a beat.

Explains Gillis in a 2009 email interview with me: "I think I've gone down a very different path from many sample-based artists in how I've released my music in that I put it out on a small indie label, and the compositions are based on so many samples. I'm not saying that it's more right or wrong than anyone else, but I think it's a difficult thing to compare to other artists. It's always a case-by-case basis."

It may be that the sampling debate in general has lost legal weight in light of the bigger concern over downloading disputes, where record labels seem to be fighting a losing battle. If Girl Talk were an African American hip hopper, might he have been an easier target, given the historical over-policing of this community and its art? When asked if there is a double standard in the copyright treatment of hip hoppers versus other genres, Gillis implies that musicians who sampled music during the 1980s in general had it tougher, and that it might not have anything to do with race or music genre.

"As we move into the future, we understand ownership of ideas differently," Gillis says. "The world understands sampling in 2009 much differently than sampling in 1988. Recontextualization of pre-existing media is a familiar element of Internet culture. Everyone was scrutinized more aggressively on this issue in the past."

Fair enough. But that's not how hip hoppers largely view modern-day sampling. The idea of them not having to pay for samples is absurd, but welcomed. What kind of message are lawmakers sending to the many rappers over the last twenty years whose careers have been derailed as a result of copyright infringement cases that have not gone in their favor, or who have had to pay large amounts of money to sample tiny bits of past popular and obscure recordings?

Chapter 3
What's Race Got to Do with It?

Hip hop is the only music genre where massive numbers of white and non-black youth of color worship the music of largely black performers. Most of the major popular rap artists celebrated worldwide are black.

As the baby boomer era enters its inevitable twilight, and hip hop's audiences diversify, rap music culture more than anything comes to represent generational changes on how we view racism. Hip hop generationers did not personally witness the struggle to abolish Jim Crow or get to weigh in on the Cuban Missile Crisis as it happened. Youth in the West in particular have matured in a universe where Asian turntablists, Latin American b-girls, aboriginal producers and continental African emcees occupy a position of influence across invisible borders.

In the US, a growing critical mass of multiculti hip hop-fuelled youth organizers created the groundswell of political activity ushering in a movement four years before Barack Obama's presidency. In 2004, I covered the first-ever National Hip Hop Political Convention in New Jersey and witnessed the Rainbow Coalition-styled organizing of youth of color who tend to be galvanized more by hip hop than by race, class or gender — all happening out of the sightlines of baby boomers.[1] Obama's presidency is no surprise to this large cadre of raptivists who've grown up seeing black people occupy new positions of power — the world's best golfer (Tiger Woods) and female tennis players (Venus and Serena Williams), the richest woman in America (billionaire Oprah Winfrey), ex-Time Warner president (Richard Parsons) and the like.

Juxtapose that with the fact that white-skinned Eminem is still the biggest-selling rapper of all time (in "White America" he admits that he can sell more CDs because of his race) coupled with the premature elevation by critics of the unquestionably average rapper Asher Roth in 2009 — and you could have a music genre following the same trajectory as other HBM (Historically Black Musics) like blues, jazz and rock'n'roll. The African American creators of these genres have largely moved on and given up ownership. For the few black performers who do still perform the blues or rock'n'roll, black audiences are scant if not non-existent. Rock'n'roll was invented and modified by black musicians Chuck Berry, Little Richard and Bo Diddley, yet Elvis Presley is considered the King of Rock, and when people think of rock music, visions of shaggy-haired, mostly Caucasian males come to mind. It's a complete rewrite of black music history.[2]

The Whitening of Rap's Audience

*I hate music where white people are trying to sound black.
The white music I like is white.*

    — Kanye West, referring to his appreciation of the
band Franz Ferdinand[3]

What is it about black music that is so attractive to non-black communities? And why do youth of all persuasions simulate the identifiably black hip hop swagger of their rap heroes like Jay-Z or Bun B in terms of walking style (gait), dress codes and slanguage? No one's sure, but some credible theories have been put forward by some credible non-black theorists.

William "Upski" Wimsatt, a modern-day John Howard Griffin (author of *Black Like Me*), minus the tanning prescriptions, is the self-published author of *Bomb the Suburbs*, a loose memoir of the white experience in rap. He also edited *How to Get Stupid White Men Out of Office*, a civic engagement-fuelled comedic spin on the more widely known movie by Michael Moore of a similar name.

Wimsatt became a cult figure among white suburban youth for helping to bridge the racial chasm with his books, and for attempting to articulate more clearly to both blacks and whites what each should learn about the other. In *Bomb*, he describes how whites live vicariously through black rappers' lives and tales, entering sexier and more stimulating environments than they would otherwise experience in the suburbs (the oft-mocked locale where it is always assumed whites live). Wimsatt's story in the *Source*, a monthly magazine at one time considered the "hip hop bible," unconsciously updates the White Negro character painted by Norman Mailer and explains why whites go out of their way to act black. He prophetically warns that whites will exploit hip hop, because his race is known for stealing and co-opting creative work.[4]

In 1991, *Newsweek* produced a sloppy cover story on the then nascent Gangsta Rap scene, citing a questionable statistic that is still being debated today. The magazine posited that 70 percent of hip hop's audience is composed of white people, who have the greatest impact on record store registers. Despite there being no real measuring stick to prove this data, the 70 percent figure gets repeated so much that it's become a reality to most.[5] And it has triggered a virtual cottage industry of pop culture produce to discuss the theory, from books like *Why White Kids Love Hip Hop* by Bakari Kitwana to the hit VH1 TV series, Ego Trip's *(White) Rapper Show*.

The problem is this theory is full of leaky holes. There is no reliable demographic study that measures hip hop's cultural or racial breakdown in areas of CD sales or live concert demographics in the US. And there is no definitive study of methodology that can measure the race of rap consumers, especially with oncoming digital distribution models. How can we possibly trace who's buying what from their Dell laptop? Also, SoundScan, an information system that is supposed to track music and music video sales in the US and Canada, doesn't include numerous venues and vehicles where rap loyalties lie — from mom-and-pop stores to bootlegged mixtape CDs to illegal downloads or discs sold out of jeep trunks.

American author Adam Mansbach (*Angry Black White Boy*) has penned some brilliant essays on the whole Wigga (white nigga) phenomenon. He believes that there is much race-baiting going on between journalists, rap fans and rappers themselves, which creates a vicious cycle of avoidance when it comes to having a healthy discussion of why race matters in American music and life.

In a 2009 email interview with me, Mansbach explains: "Hip hop is America's de facto youth culture, so it's inevitably consumed by more white kids than black, resulting in a situation where the entire industry tacitly agrees to pretend that hip hop is created for and by 'the streets,' i.e., the black streets, and that anybody else listening in is a voyeur. Financially, that doesn't compute, but it preserves an illusion that is profitable, and it also allows corporations to avoid responsibility for violent or misogynist content by saying (to paraphrase Russell Simmons) 'these are just guys from the 'hood, telling their own stories for their people.' Of course, when content becomes offensive to a white corporate sensibility (i.e., 'Cop Killer'), it's a different story; it gets shut down with the quickness."

Due to the severe mainstreaming of hip hop culture over the last decade, Mansbach believes that white youth might no longer feel the need to have any real contact with the black communities who create the music, because now they "feel invested in hip hop, feel the right to claim it, partly because they have invested their money, their time."

He explains: "You've got a huge generational shift in terms of how hip hop is consumed — from underground to overground, from in person to virtually — and what it means in terms of race is that white kids don't have to ever be in black spaces, don't even have to be in the minority, don't have to contend with whether they're trespassing by participating in hip hop, because they're doing it all from the privacy of their homes. Or they can become part of insular all-white hip hop communities; there didn't use to be enough white listeners for that to happen. So the upshot of it all is that hip hop, in the last fifteen years, has gone from being one of the only sites in American life where…white kids were forced to think about race, privilege and appropriation to a space where white entitlement remains intact and goes unchallenged."

Debates around cultural ownership are important to hip hop, given the fact that African American culture has suffered a long history of exploitation for others' gain — and there should be great concern that hip hop is next on the list. Culture is a funny thing in that it is not something that can be controlled and locked in the basement. Culture travels at the speed of light (or Internet cable lines) and doesn't respect borders. If some youth in the Ukraine sees someone speed-rapping on his or her MTV subsidiary and enjoys it, he or she could conceivably begin to mimic these rap styles, and before you know it, there's a high energy crunk rap scene with an accompanying repetitive chorus in Kiev. (Crunk is a style of Southern rap music featuring repetitive chants and rapid dance rhythms.)

Hip hop is for everybody. But every hip hop practitioner needs to understand how hip hop got to the place it is today, and what it means to the people who invented the art form. Mansbach points out that "no high school kid today, unless he or she does serious research, is going to connect hip hop with social protest or political struggle, even though it was born out of that. On the contrary, commercial hip hop has become proof for a lot of white kids who have no contact with black people that blacks actually have it better than they do: they're cooler, they've got cars and women and jewelry, the ghetto is a nonstop party interrupted occasionally by gunfire."

What a community creates cannot be bought and sold to the highest bidders with no regard to the creators and originators. One hundred years from now will black people be on the outside, looking in at a hip hop culture they invented that carries few black performers and even fewer audience members? Will they be scratching their heads in disbelief, mocked like Little Richard is when he claims to be the real king of rock'n'roll — which he is?

N Bomb

Warning. Before reading this section, I offer the faint of heart this advice: take a nice, deep breath. Put down that tea and toast for a second. Faggot. Retard. Cracker. Nigger. After reading these words, does your body have a negative physiological response? Can you even say these words without feeling queasy or that you did something wrong? That's precisely the reason the N-word should be removed from all rap albums, like a virus from your computer.

The bottom line is this. The N-word might be the most offensive expletive on the planet. And if not for hip hop culture, where the use of the word is a widespread salutation, there would be no discussion of it here. You would be hard-pressed to find another music genre carrying artists that routinely issue the expletive — the word is uttered a nauseating 249 times on rap legend N.W.A.'s (Niggaz With Attitude) platinum-selling *Efil4zaggin* album. That's more usage of the word than at a Klu Klux Klan rally. The word should have gone the way of disco — dead.

The widespread use of the loaded term has triggered much debate. Should only blacks use it? Should it be banned altogether? Is saying "nigga," instead of "nigger," a genuine re-branding and reclamation of the loaded term? When KRS-One rapped, "now we got white kids calling themselves nigga," he expressed surprise at how often the term is being used by Caucasian youth. But what would he have to say about the use of the word by Latino rappers and fans who are either products of miscegenation and/or have obvious black African bloodlines? From American-based politico rapper Immortal Technique to rhyme kingpin B-Real (Cypress Hill) and Fat Joe — all are light-skinned Latinos who have used the word in their rhymes as a term of endearment. Why then should the formerly hip hop-affiliated R&B singer

Jennifer Lopez AKA J-Lo get bashed by critics for using the same word in her 2001 remix single "I'm Real"? Is it less okay for light-skinned Latina women to use it than men? Is it okay for non-black Latinos to use it, period?

The bigger problem arises when non-Westerners get broadcast feeds of rappers uttering the N-word. They have no context or history behind the term, so they simply repeat it. For example, in Malawi, there is a hip hop clothing store called Nigger, because the owners equate it with a term of endearment for African American rappers.

Why a call for the abolition of the word?[6] It's really simple. It was invented by racist whites who lynched black people because of the color of their skin at a time when the KKK ran rampant, when blacks were not allowed to drink at the same water fountain or use the same washrooms as whites. Do we need any more reasons? It's the near identical reason that Chinese do not want to call each other Chinks or Jews call each other kikes or Pakistanis call each other Pakis — it's all hurtful, offensive language invented by cultural outsider groups to do just that. Offend.

Some rappers or rap fans support the continued use of the word with a different spelling (with an "a" suffix as opposed to an "er" suffix), arguing that it takes on a different meaning, a "taking back" of the term, and that only blacks can use it as insider language. But they have missed the larger point. Language can't be owned or captured by any community. It travels the globe via the web, TV and print, and gets picked up by citizens of all nations.

Many rappers severely underestimate the power of

their words and their impact globally. It took one trip to Kenya in 1979 by renowned comedian Richard Pryor — a regular user of the word during his routines — for him to grasp the impact of anti-black racism on diasporic black communities. Pryor renounced his own use of the term after having an epiphany in his hotel room. And besides, anyone who thinks it's worth advocating for continued use of the N-word probably has too much time on their hands, time better spent lobbying for more worthwhile causes like ending child poverty or homelessness.

Major corporations are complicit in the production and distribution of the N-word, because they are the ones who are funding the CDs' creation. It's simple. If Universal, Sony BMG, EMI/Virgin agreed not to sign and release any music that features this language because it's offensive, it would effectively stop most rappers using the terminology. Where's the corporate responsibility?

When legendary rapper Nas made the decision to release his tenth studio album and call it *Nigger* (the title ultimately got kiboshed by his label due to public pressure), was it a publicity ploy, career desperation or an exercise by Nas to see how far his label Sony BMG was willing to go?[7] I think that Nas could have come up with another title by tapping into his creativity and wit. It's a bit artless not to use other language like "brother" (nigga, when used by rappers, is supposed to be a substitute for "friend" or "brother"), a word with no venom. The late Tupac Shakur, who subverted the word to be used as an acronym for "Never Ignorant about Getting Goals Accomplished," was more crafty.

Blaming hip hop is not what's needed in any analysis of the N-word's use. Non-black popular culture has always spread and awarded use of the N-word, from Mark Twain's widely read *Huckleberry Finn* to Harper Lee's Pulitzer Prize-winning *To Kill a Mockingbird*. To Twain apologists, I say, at least the KKK had the smarts to hide underneath sheets. The problem today is that hip hop exists in a digital era where words spread a lot faster around the world over Internet cable lines. I'd like to think that rappers don't mean any harm using the word, but they *are* unconsciously harming people with its use.

There shouldn't be much of an N-word debate today. It should be removed from the music and mouths of all rap babes. The CDs of artless artists who can't come up with any other creative wordplay are deserving of frisbee or drink coaster status. Free speech is what's needed in this world, and censorship of music is not always a good thing. But where do we draw the line? It's not okay to publicly express and act out one's hatred for women on a CD. So hip hop needs to put "nigga" to rest, the way the NAACP (National Association for the Advancement of Colored People) did. They staged a mock burial of the word — coffin, cemetery and all — in 2007.[8] And at the wake, we can have an open discussion about why it went six feet under.

Post-Apartheid Voices

South African rap is a distinctive cultural byproduct of post-apartheid sensibilities. (Apartheid was the South African government-sanctioned racial segregation between 1949 and 1990 that severely impacted black communities.) In the much-ballyhooed dawn of a "new" South Africa, where the races are now supposed to be intermingling freely and blacks are supposed to be sharing in the resources robbed from them by racist colonizers, rap music has emerged as a speak-out mechanism for youth and young adults.

South Africa (in particular Cape Town, Pretoria and Johannesburg) is not only the site of one of the most active hip hop scenes in all of Africa, it is also one of the oldest scenes, as South Africa was one of the first African countries to have consistent contact with the US and access to its music. Music has always played a strong role in the struggle against apartheid, as the film *Amandla!* (power) documented. It was a tool that brought oppressed blacks from Soweto and other townships across the country into a united front of harmonious protest. Rap music now provides a nouveau outlet for social messages in a more urgent, critical fashion. It is used as a tool to get out important messages about HIV and AIDS, for example. (An estimated 13 percent of forty-three million South Africans are infected with HIV.)[9]

Kwaito, a freakish hybrid music form developed by post-apartheid South Africans that blends the full range of the black music spectrum — disco, rap, rhythm and blues, reggae and house music, mixed in with indigenous music and rhymes — has captured the imagination of youth. Kwaito describes the complexities and contradictions of growing up in a traditional music setting coupled

Tumi and the Volume

Tumi Molekane (Boitumelo Molekane) is one of South Africa's most talented rap voices. In the new South Africa, blacks, whites and Asians generally don't intermingle, but don't tell that to this black Muslim rapper. Tumi raps mostly in English, and his Volume band features white South African Jewish bassist Dave Bergman, a Muslim drummer and Mozambican multi-instrumentalists Tiago Paulo and Paulo Chibanga. His rap verses wax poignantly about daily life in Johannesburg.[10]

What role do post-apartheid feelings among South African citizens play in the creation of contemporary rap music?

We make music in a post-apartheid atmosphere that might be similar to what happens in these post-colonial African countries. That said, this is uncharted terrain for us. All these truths revealing themselves have a clear sway on the music. Well for one, the depoliticized mood of the people reflects in the kind of music that people want to hear.

Are youth in South Africa reflecting their own local area concerns in their rhymes or rapping about stuff they see happening in America and abroad via CNN?

They are reflecting their own experiences. Living in the ghettoes, coming from apartheid, getting paid, the promise of wealth, and because they make hip hop music, the American influence is there. If they do care what is going on in the dirty South or LA, it's mostly to draw inspiration from their successful counterparts. In many ways, the aspirations of these young rappers from the States is similar to that of young South Africans. Black people in the States are the wealthiest and most visible in the world today — why wouldn't we draw from them? If you study African political development, you will see the parallels between, say, negritude and black nationalism.

Does your music get the support of the corporations or record labels in South Africa? Does it matter?

Well, every album I have done with the band or solo has been nominated for a South African music award. It matters because you must exist. The people you are trying to speak to love the pharaoh, and they are not trying to hear you from outside the palace. So we venture through the gates sometimes, although the only way is to build our own institutions, which is hard considering most people are politically hung over and are trying to get a piece of this "freedom" rationed out.

Has the Internet helped or harmed you and the wider South African hip hop creation and salability?

I want to speak to the world through my art and the world has shrunk to a nutshell now (because of the Internet). I am trying to find ways of getting people the music for free. South Africans still buy music cause the digital revolution is more of an evolution back home. I don't have a problem with people wanting my music and downloading it out there or sharing it with each other. I do however have a problem with low-quality bootlegs and edited pirated stuff – that's not how you intended your music to sound like.

What does the future of South African-produced rap music look like?

The hip hop scene in South Africa will continue to grow. I would love to see it develop into a cultural force and embrace its revolutionary roots so as to inspire and accelerate positive change.

with post-apartheid Internet and satellite television access and it questions South African traditions more than any previous generation's music.

Reservation Rap

In 2006, Canada's aboriginal population topped the one million mark for the first time, a dramatic rise of 45 percent from the previous decade.[11] Why should you care? Well, for a few Notorious B.I.G. reasons. Rap's claim to be a voice of disenfranchised youth and a vehicle that puts a mirror to harsh realities could not have found a more ideal constituency, one that rivals only African people in its history of displacement and colonization.

It is rap music that has largely captured the senses of this young community, whose average age is twenty-five years old (compared to the average age of forty of the non-aboriginal population).

When NYC-based rapper KRS-One, the most prolific emcee of our time, rapped on "Sound of Da Police" that "there could never really be justice on stolen land," one can only speculate whether he knew about what was happening up North. From the Ojibway, Dene and Inuit communities to the Algonquian, Iroquois and Cree settlements across Canada, the tales of strife of Canada's original peoples ring as true as, if not more true, than hip hop's black founding fathers. One-half of the community live on reserves — a piece of land that is dedicated to a band — and the conditions in which large chunks of the community live, in what can be considered rural 'hoods, rival those of the urban 'hoods you hear about in thousands of rap songs. And in the same way that the analog or digital African drum rhythm finds its way onto many rap tracks, the drum is central to most native communities and ceremonies. It is considered by many to be the heartbeat of the Earth. Blending native voices and rhythms makes up the core of traditional aboriginal music, so it is really no surprise that hip hop has become the voice of aboriginal youth in Canada.

None of this is lost on groundbreaking aboriginal rap group War Party. Formed in 1995, War Party is in the vanguard of the Canadian aboriginal rap scene, and serves as a role model that deserves a lot more mention as revolutionary Canadian rappers. Led by a married couple from Hobbema, Alberta, Rex and Cynthia Smallboy, War Party is driven to change the way Canadian society looks at aboriginal people, not only by rapping but by conducting workshops on substance abuse and native cultural uplift. The group's breakthrough album, *The Reign* (2000), was released to critical acclaim and it is the first aboriginal rap group to receive funding from VideoFACT— a granting program operated by Canada's equivalent to MTV and MuchMusic — which supplies non-recoupable monies to artists. Rex Smallboy, who's lost a few relatives to suicide, believes rap provided a much-needed creative outlet to escape harsh realities when he was a young man growing up in Alberta. In a 2008 interview he told me: "I related to the frustration and anger in the (rap) music and it made me want to stand up for my people like they were…. It is what youth relate to, and we need to teach them their true identity somehow."

Having recorded with rap's most poignant voice, Chuck D of Public Enemy, War Party has transcended native boundaries, connecting like-intentioned, politically conscious wordsmiths to transmit messages of native uplift, cross-culturally and nationally.

The Tru Rez Crew from Six Nations Reserve in Ontario (a three-hour drive from Toronto) are also seasoned hip hop veterans. Saskatchewan's award-winning Reddnation group (featuring members from Edmonton, Alberta, and Regina, Saskatchewan) received two grants from MuchMusic's VideoFACT program, for video singles "Fabulous" and "Wiggle Dem Toes."

Penticton, BC's 7th Generation, repeat Canadian Aboriginal Music Award recipient, has been working hard to create a rap world in which it is cool to learn how to breakdance and grass dance, to powwow and produce hot beats simultaneously. Says rapper Kasp from 7th Generation in an online interview with me in 2009: "In the aboriginal community you see a lot of young people who still have a strong connection with traditional music.... There is definitely a combination of hip hop and aboriginal tradition in the smaller communities, more so than in the bigger cities where the ties to traditional ways are not as prominent."

Kasp goes so far as to make a direct link between black American rap traits and traditional indigenous cultures: "The reservation is like the (American) ghetto, and the ghetto is like the reservation. The four elements of hip hop and the elements of aboriginal culture are very similar. Powwow dancing is the same as b-boying, emceeing is like storytelling and powwow songs. Graffiti is like aboriginal art and deejaying is like the powwow drum…they all express themselves through those forms and tell their story through those forms."

Hip hop's inherent "voice for the voiceless" protest ethic leaves its aboriginal youth practitioners with feelings of being less Reserved. Hip hop helps heal the psychic wounds of racism and silence passed down from generations of native Canadians who suffered physical, emotional and sexual abuse at the hands of church officials who operated assimilationist government-funded residential schools.[12] As rapper Hellnback, from all-star aboriginal rap collective Team Rezofficial puts it, "Hip hop, to me, has been the biggest therapist in my life."[13]

Country music, blues and folk music have always had a strong foothold in Canadian aboriginal communities, but for some of the new school of native youth, listening to the blues is about as exciting as watching the Olympics' synchronized swimming finals. Rap music works as the perfect vehicle for marginalized rural aboriginal youth to express themselves. Utilizing inexpensive recording software that doesn't require years of study to master or any vocal training, rap is the most accessible, democratized music form. But as in any musical or cultural community, one can't expect all aboriginal rappers to speak out against issues related to racism, assimilation or land claims. Apolitical party raps that celebrate life's great pleasures can also act as a catharsis for wordsmiths whose daily realities aren't so good.

On the flipside, can hip hop have the opposite effect

and inspire violence and drug use, the same things it was intended to speak out against? This is a trend that could have a crippling effect on historically disadvantaged communities. Says Smallboy, "Shit, on my rez there is like drive-by shootings. I know a lot of youth looked up to Dr. Dre when he dropped *The Chronic* and Master P made them try to cook crack. I know firsthand how it has an effect." He adds, "That is why we need to focus on building up their true identity so they will be stronger in the choices they make."

7th Generation's Zane believes that the correlation between bad art and youth acting out can be real: "Thug rap music definitely plays a negative role and anyone who says that it doesn't influence young, confused youth who are looking for their own identity to relate to haven't been that youth." He adds that the mainstream media's promotion of negative raps to meet bottom lines is what might win out if indigenous youth aren't media savvy.

But the upsurge in interest among youth looking to rally around a shared new music and culture won't be slowing down any time soon. The first First Nations Hip Hop Festival was held in 2004 on the Pasqua First Nation near Fort Qu'Appelle, Saskatchewan. It featured provincial-area acts, including Wake MC, Pasqua Breakers and DJ Roxy Princess. Regina rapper Anish of the Pasqua First Nation organized the festival because she wanted to provide youth with a "chance to create and recreate their own sense of identity."[14]

Following on the heels of these energies, in 2008 the federal government funded the Kivalliq Inuit Association project that links local area youth and rap music with elders and throat singers as a means to connect their language and cultural identity through popular music. Likewise, the *Beat Nation — Hip Hop as an Indigenous Culture* art exhibit at the SAW Gallery in Ottawa in April 2009 was the first to fully showcase a new generation of artists who project the influence of rap music and graffiti culture on traditional aboriginal life.

High-profile rap critics are looking closely at Team Rezofficial — a Canadian aboriginal rap super group with members from all over the prairies — to turn up the heat and progress the scene. Technological advances have made it easier for them to record and share music online, without having to be physically on the same reserve. They aim to raise the quality of native rap and escape the pigeonholing and novelty of being considered simply aboriginal rappers. As Team Rez founder Stomp says in an interview on the influential hiphopcanada.com site, "We've never been big on coming out there and saying we're Native, we're Native, we're Native — and it's not because we're not proud of it, we are proud of it — but we'd rather be seen as musicians first."[15]

Rap Slanguage

Unless you live on Pluto, in a crater, or with earplugs stuffed into your auditory canal, you've heard someone utter the term "baby mama" to describe a young mother.

How exactly did baby mama become a household phrase? And how did unpopular ex-presidents begin to greet other heads of state with "Yo"?[16]

Portrait of Paniccioli

One of hip hop culture's first and maybe its most important photographer is an American Indian named Ernie Paniccioli. A proud Cree, Paniccioli says very few people ever ask him about his background.

"When people do figure it out, and ask me what reservation I'm from, I tell 'em Brooklyn," explains the crafty lens man at an interview I conducted with him in New York in 2008. "One of the problems I had growing up was that I was surrounded by a multicultural group of people," says the self-taught photographer, whose first book *Who Shot Ya?* and eight subsequent books run the gamut of hip hop-friendly counterculture from early celebrity headshots to nascent punk music scenes all the way to graffiti culture documentation. "The Hispanic kids thought I was Hispanic, but I didn't speak the language, so they thought I was being arrogant and they used to beat my ass. The Italian kids saw my last name and with that I was considered a half-breed and they hated that and they would beat my ass."

His early alignment with black people and their culture came as a result of, uhh...not getting beat down by them? "When I was ten years old, I was getting the beat down by some white kids, and all I saw was black hands and black fists coming in to defend me. These three black kids beat down ten white kids. From that day onwards I was a member of an all-black gang in Brooklyn called the Bishops. Black people were the only group that never gave me any trouble racially, partially because they were too busy with life, occupied with basic shit like trying to eat."

Brother Ernie, the "Indian guy who was always trying to take your picture even when you didn't want it taken," as broadcast iconoclasts Ed Lover and Dr. Dre put it, has been photographing hip hop culture since the early 1970s. In 1973, he began documenting the graffiti art scene in NYC with his trusty 35-millimeter camera.

Paniccioli is often compared to African American documentary photographer James Van Der Zee, who singularly managed to capture the Harlem Renaissance of the 1920s, or to American Edward S. Curtis, whose documentation of the native people of North America offers up some of the only recorded history of a similarly marginalized group. Paniccioli has recorded the entire evolution of this outlaw music and culture called hip hop. Just check out the photo credits on many of the seminal images that have gone into high circulation, from the celebrated Rock Steady Crew breakdancing and Grandmaster Flash rocking out at the Roxy (a trendy Manhattan nightclub of the 1970s and early 1980s) to arguably rap's greatest emcees Tupac Shakur and the Notorious B.I.G. and femcee Lauryn Hill.

Ernie witnessed firsthand the rock'n'roll inventions of Little Richard and Chuck Berry, and knew there was something special about this nascent cultural movement. Some of these special feelings are fading, he admits. And it's not about his age or generation — it's because he expected forty years after the music's invention that it would embrace more of its original activist leanings.

"I've spent four decades documenting hip hop, but before I am a hip hop photographer, I am a man, and I stand up for what I believe in. If you don't stand for something, you will fall for anything," he says, referencing his mother's teachings about nature and Cree spirituality that drive him. "Hip hop was originally a voice of the voiceless, it was a voice of the solution, and now it's become the problem, a capitalistic tool to sell all types of things we don't need. Cars, cereal, alcohol and junk food. Diddy and Jay-Z with all their fame are pushing alcohol and vodka, and if you know about First Nations, that's killed more people than guns or anything else. It's gone from us being spiritual forces to gun clapping and booty shaking."

He adds: "If hip hop is a culture, like many like to claim, then where is our hip hop museum, school, political movement, hospital? Do 50 Cent or Russell Simmons, two multimillionaires, have any interest in getting together to start hip hop health insurance programs or anti-gang initiatives and all those other things that would truly make us a culture? I have my doubts."

Hip hop aficionados are giving Paniccioli his long overdue credit. He was immortalized in a 2007 documentary directed by Dion Ashman, *The Other Side of Hip Hop: The Sixth Element*, which details the life, struggles, politics and work of this longtime hip hop photo activist. "Better late than never," he says.

Anyone who's listened to the speech patterns of your average teenager lately will notice that they *do* speak a different language than most of their school teachers. "Bling bling" is now a universal salutation that youth from Japan to Jordan know means "flashy," and everybody from baby boomers to out-of-touch suburbanite soccer moms and CNN broadcasters want to get jiggy with it (get involved with it).

Okay, so the word jiggy is so played out it should be put in a time capsule along with Atari game consoles. But no one knows how we got to a place where rap's esoteric linguistic code has infiltrated the White House and corporate boardrooms. What we do know is that it isn't new for youth to have their own jargon. Blues music artists of the early 1900s developed a whole lexicon of words like mojo (charm used against someone else) or boogie (to move or dance quickly) that are still used today.

How did rappers form their own vocabulary? It finds its lineage in Ebonics, the lay term for the language spoken by African Americans that has strong African retentions, or what linguists call AAVE (African American Vernacular English). To the surprise of many who assume that the "King's English" is the only "proper" English, educators like Michael Eric Dyson have long argued that much African American dialect used in hip hop is a language related to West African languages, and was used by slaves in the American South so they would not be understood by slave masters. Hip hoppers re-invigorated this type of linguistic trickery so they would not be understood by their parents.

Dyson and others argued that the way some African American children speak when they show up in schools is so different from standard English that teachers often can't understand what they are saying. These children often perform poorly in school and fail to acquire the ways of speaking that they'll need in order to succeed in the world outside their neighborhoods. In 1996-97, a debate in the school district in Oakland, California, centered around whether Ebonics or AAVE should be given some institutional merit as a legitimate "language," and whether lesson plans in this language should be included in teachers' curriculums. While there was a resolution to have the language recognized as a legitimate African American language to be learned and taught, that motion was subsequently dropped in favor of more ongoing debates about how to address this heated issue that the community itself is divided on.

By the late 1990s, hip hop's impact was being felt everywhere. By 2000, with the inclusion of jiggy — taken from a rhyme from the Grammy-winning Fresh Prince — in the Oxford English Dictionary, the literary floodgates seemed to burst wide open with the possibility that hip hop-informed words could be given serious consideration for inclusion into these holy texts.

How do words that seem like castaways, bad language, or even worse — slang — get considered for inclusion in prestigious tomes like the Oxford English Dictionary? For starters, at Oxford online, a new term that is under consideration is furiously researched by staffers and has to appear in printed reading materials at least twenty-five times. Citations should come from a credible range of periodicals that have fair circulation.

In 2003, the Oxford English Dictionary added "bling bling," a phrase invented and popularized by New Orleans-based rapper B.G., describing it as a term that means "flashy accessories."[17] B.G., the word's creator, in true capitalist rap fashion, had this to say: "I just wish that I'd trademarked it, so I'd never have to work again."[18]

Others like Atlanta-based rapper Lil Jon were even more elated when their vernacular made it to the literary promised land. In 2007, "crunk" was added to the Merriam-Webster's Collegiate Dictionary, joining terms like "bootylicious." Lil Jon is the lone creator and promoter of crunk music and crunk juice (an energy drink) — the word refers to "a style of southern rap music featuring repetitive chants and rapid dance rhythms."[19]

The tricky part about recording the words that the hip hop nation understands and uses is that they are constantly being upgraded and re-invented by a bevy of personalities across the United States. Oakland, California's E-40, credited with coining a large number of terms of everyday hip hop use like "shizzle" (for sure) or "po-po" (police) seems to add new slanguage to the rap vocabulary with every CD he releases.

Pioneering music journalist and ex-*Vibe* magazine columnist Bonz Malone punctuates all of his words that end in the letter "s" with "z," among other tricks, inspiring teens worldwide to write like this (e.g., "sticks and stones" becomes "stickz and stonez").

To keep up with hip hop-fuelled language formation

amongst urban youth, a virtual cottage industry of guide-books has cropped up to capture this living, breathing, rapidly shifting language. From the seminal 1995 *A 2 Z: The Book of Rap and Hip Hop Slang* to *Hip Hoptionary: The Dictionary of Hip Hop Terminology*, all the way to newer similarly themed titles like *Street Talk: Da Official Guide to Hip Hop and Urban Slanguage* and *Mo' Urban Dictionary: Ridonkulous Street Slang Defined*, hip hop lan-guage has infiltrated mainstream youth culture expres-sion in a major way. And an Encyclopedia Raptanica may soon be on its way.

Corporate America is certainly listening. In 2002, in CNN's aim to attract younger audiences in the eighteen to thirty-five-year-old range — who are generally consid-ered more attractive to advertisers because of their spend-ing habits — the broadcasters seamlessly mixed in hip hop phrases like "flava" and "fly" (both words mean "good') in their daily newscasts, sending a clear message that rap slanguage is the currency to engage youth audiences.

The practitioners and icons of hip hop-driven vocab-ulary have not only composed their own lingua for use in their own insider subcultural group, but their wordplay has entered the wider non-hip hop culture slang canon. For example, "mullet" is a word used to describe a hair-style worn mostly by men in which the hair is cut short at the front and sides and left long in the back. Arguably the most ridiculed hairdo of all time, "mullet" was popu-larized by US hip hop group the Beastie Boys on their 1994 "Mullet Head" song from their *Tour Shot!* album.

Hip hop slanguage is used everywhere — in standard

English dictionaries and in classrooms. But when a word is being utilized by stiff-suited CNN anchors who are twice the age of your average hip hopper, it also means that the word will be so mainstream that the same rap subgroup that created it will promptly remove it from the good books — it will have become officially lame. And then the culture's wordsmiths will move on and create new terms. A rigorous counterculture like hip hop relies on witty insider language to separate its practitioners and fans from the monotonous, banal world of the "normals" — your parents and the suburbs.

Hip Hop Hoorays and Handshakes

Not only do hip hoppers speak a different language, but they greet one another differently too. So what's in a greeting, you say? Apparently plenty, if you're a part of that hip hop aesthetic that forsakes handshakes for exchanging "some skin." Instead of performing stiff, upright handshakes in school or work scenarios, hip hoppers prefer to give their homeboys and girls (friends) a "pound." Giving the proverbial handslap to a friend is a hip hop-esque behavioral trait that's become second nature and works like a signifier of an unspoken code for global b-boys and girls. By giving a complete stranger one of a variety of hip hop handshakes, from a "dap," where you grip palms lightly and then end with a finger snap, to a "pound," where loosely clenched fists come crashing together softly — you are displaying a symbol of group belonging, affection and togetherness. These days, hip hop heads not only clutch and grab palm surfaces — as stiff opposition to even stiffer handshakes — but they also hug one another, acting out what is known as the Hip Hop Hug.

Chapter 4
Hip Hop's Economic Stimulus Plan

*See now I take trips to Baghdad/Use a stack of chips to count
Arab money now/I don't need to get fresh, I'm 'bout to grow
a beard dude/So much cake even the money look weird
too...We gettin' Arab money, We gettin' Arab money!*
— Busta Rhymes, "Arab Money"

There is no other music genre in the history of North
American music that is as fixated on money as hip hop.
Making it, spending it, flaunting it. Some of the best-
selling and most integral rap songs of all time are explic-
itly about money: Diddy's "It's All About the
Benjamins," Eric B and Rakim's "Paid in Full." There
are dozens of other chart-topping groups that rap about
their favorite green things — that ain't Kermit or envy —
or are named after money and refer specifically to large
amounts of it, like Cash Money Millionaires,
Chamillionaire, or EPMD (Erick and Parrish Making
Dollars).

In hip hop circles, the debate is not about "selling
out," but about how to buy in to the Machine. Make no

mistake, a large element of contemporary commercial rap music is about excess and living large.

Lords of the Bling

What is it exactly about cash that turns hip hop's crank?

When you turn on your favorite video networks, MTV, BET, MuchMusic or VH1, it's no coincidence that most contemporary hip hop videos feature rappers flaunting what they believe to be accessories of the "good life": money, fast cars, mansions and jewelry. The argument goes that rappers originally became obsessed with making lots of money and living extravagantly as a byproduct of growing up in low-income environments. That is, when a kid grows up in a housing project and is never able to afford a new pair of Nikes, when he does get some money, he buys not one, but twelve pairs of those same shoes. The funny thing is, rap went from being America's broke urban youth voice and unifying force, neither lucrative nor popular in the late 1970s, to a multibillion dollar industry.

A sign of just how corporate the multibillion dollar hip hop industry has become is that the usually stiff and stodgy *Forbes* magazine produces a list devoted entirely to the world's wealthiest rappers. Master P and P. Diddy have shown up on its ranking of the world's highest money earners, clocking over $50 million in annual earnings, despite being bred in poor neighborhoods in New Orleans (Magnolia Projects) and New York (Harlem), respectively. The top spot in Forbes' 20 Richest Rappers 2008 list went to 50 Cent with his $150 million in earnings.[1]

The difference between the profit margins of today's artists and those of yesteryear is dramatic. The new rapreneurs understand their net worth and often only strike recording contracts with labels that give them a more equitable share of the profits in creative distribution deals than those who went before them. For example, Ronald (Slim) and his younger brother rapper/entrepreneur Bryan (Baby) Williams' Cash Money Records' distribution deal with Universal Motown allows them to retain ownership of their master recordings and receive a considerable chunk of their publishing and royalty revenue, something that was unheard of for artists before the new millennium.

Money Stereotypes

With the wholesale hip hop pursuit of getting Donald Trump-wealthy, sometimes promoting Western rap's capitalist dogma to non-Western cultural ears goes awfully awry. In 2008, Busta Rhymes' "Arab Money" song and video featured him perpetuating crude stereotypes about Arab communities and wealth. The video shows Busta hanging out in Arab oil fields and walking through palatial estates, while making half-baked lyrical references to facial hair worn by Muslims ("about to grow a beard dude") and wanting "oil well money." Busta subsequently pulled his song after talking to Montreal-based Iraqi-Canadian rapper The Narcicyst, whose song "Real Arab Money" challenged this stereotypical view of his culture.

The fact is, there are Arabs who aren't Muslims and Muslims who aren't Arabs, and Arab countries with no oil resources. While "Arab Money" did much to refuel stereotypes the Arab community has been trying to rid itself of for decades, and reflects a lack of understanding of some of the real facts about Arab life, this controversy provided a much-needed opportunity for Arab rappers like The Narcicyst to educate non-Arabs about the tenets of their culture.

Simmons Lathan Media Group (SLMG), a company that studies and distributes youth market content reports that rap's American customer base is made up of 45 million hip hop consumers between the ages of 13 and 34 — 80 percent of whom are white. This group now has over $1 trillion in spending power.[2]

Though beats and rhymes are their specialty, young rap entrepreneurs have figured out other ways to get even richer, based on the popularity of their brand names. As record sales continue to plummet because of computer downloading, rappers are acting in blockbuster movies (e.g., rapper Will Smith is one of the top three gate receipt-generating actors of all time), producing clothing lines (Nelly's Apple Bottoms) and have their own soft drinks (Lil Jon's Crunk Juice). Rapper Snoop Dogg has made wads of cash from every non-music career angle imaginable, with his own TV show (*Doggy Fizzle Televizzle*), pornographic videos (*Snoop Dogg's Doggystyle*), apparel company (Snoop Dogg Clothing) and dozens of acting credits (Starsky and Hutch). And all of this is coming from a former incarcerated drug dealer.

Fashion: The Sixth Element

Fashion has become the extra income earner of choice for hip hopreneurs because unique dress codes have always defined members of this subculture. When *Gentlemen's Quarterly* magazine crowned rapper Andre 3000 one of the five Best New Designers in early 2009 for his preppy Benjamin Bixby line, it was a clear sign that hip hop's influence on the world of high fashion is

50 Cent or 50 Million

The list of black Horatio Algers grows by the year, and no rapper around the world embodies this rag-to-riches ethos more than 50 Cent, who might need to change his rap alias to $50 million.

50 Cent is the entrepreneur's entrepreneur and might have more revenue streams than any other musician. Not bad for a guy who grew up rough in Jamaica, then lived in Queens in the midst of the 1980s crack epidemic. His mother, a drug dealer, was murdered when he was eight. Soon after, he began running cocaine for his uncles, was shot nine times and left for dead in front of his grandmother's house.

Ranking #8 on the Forbes 2006 Celebrity 100 list (#26 in 2008), here's a snapshot of his diversified financial portfolio.

Music — He has five albums, two *Billboard* #1s and over 25 million units sold worldwide.

Sex toys — His own brand name condom, the Magic Stick Lifestyles condom, is named after his song of the same name.

Beverage — Formula 50 flavor of Glaceau Vitamin Water earned $100 million when Coca Cola bought the parent company in which he had a minority stake.

Gaming — A video game, *50 Cent: Bulletproof*, and its 2009 Xbox 360 sequel, *Blood on the Sand*, are named after him

Record label — His G-Unit record label releases Lloyd Banks, Tony Yayo and Mobb Deep.

Clothing company — His G-Unit clothes gross $20 million a year in sales.

Footwear — He had his own Reebok G-Unit imprint.

Film — He has a 2005 autobiographical film, *Get Rich or Die Trying*, acting gigs in *Righteous Kill* alongside Al Pacino and Robert DeNiro, and an indie film company, Untamed Beauty.

TV — His *50 Cent: The Money and the Power* MTV reality TV series features him giving away $100,000 to the next generation of hip hopreneurs.

not some passing fancy. Fashion designer P. Diddy, a winner of the Top Menswear Designer of the Year award from the Council of Fashion Designers of America, has a large built-in audience of fans who've already bought his recordings.[3] There are others like him.

When more established American clothing brands like Tommy Hilfiger saw the spending potential of this hip, urban market in the early 1990s, they started catering to it. The formula was simple: the bigger hip hop gets, the more money one can make dressing up youth to look like their rap heroes. And the bigger the logos and color schemes, the bigger the bottom lines.

Most of *your* favorite rappers of today and yesteryear, including Nelly, T.I., Jay-Z, Eminem, Common, Young Jeezy, Eve, Busta Rhymes, Lupe Fiasco, Missy Elliott, Mos Def and Wu-Tang Clan either have their own clothing lines or peddle footwear. Hip hop culture impresario Russell Simmons first understood the link between fashion and rap when he started up his Phat Farm clothing line in 1992 (he sold his company for $140 million to Kellwood LLC in 2004).

Some issues have popped up regarding the morality behind the clothing cash grab. For example, P. Diddy has come under fire for having his company's Sean John sweatshirts produced in Honduran sweatshops. P. Diddy and Sean John executives claim to have had no knowledge of factory conditions, although the National Labor Committee report that implicated him is based on testimony by the factory workers themselves. These claims haven't done anything to slow down his hustle, as Sean

John Inc. purchased popular urban lifestyle brand Enyce in late 2008 from Liz Claiborne Inc.

The logos of Sean John, Baby Phat and Rocawear clothing lines have become as instantly recognizable as the Nike swoosh or an American flag. Authors like Naomi Klein criticize this type of branding. In her influential book *No Logo*, Klein argues that this American excess creates developing world duress "not because there's anything intrinsically wrong with logos, but because brands are developed — and their logos are designed — to market products that are produced through the exploitation and impoverishment of workers and communities in the poorest parts of the world."[4]

In the West, many fashion stereotypes are associated with your typical hip hopper. From baggy clothes and flashy jewel-encrusted accessories to rocking retro sneakers, this caricature makes rap fashionistas appear like empty consumerism-obsessed vehicles with more interest in Converse Chuck Taylors (i.e., basketball shoes) than college.

But what might make critics reconsider their jihad against rap fashionistas are the facts. The reality is that hip hop fashion styles are not arbitrary closet selections, but sometimes carefully calculated decisions rooted in class struggle and community empowerment. Next to beat boxing, fashion is one of the often overlooked aspects of hip hop, and it carries a deep, rich history. The bottom line for all aspects of the culture, given its poor working-class origins, is to make the most out of limited resources, and in fashion it's no different.

Clothes express individuality, but the fashion staples that show up in global youth culture dress codes usually have a functional or political purpose. The wearing of baggy oversized clothes is rooted in 1970s African American and Latin American New York City households where disposable income restrictions dictated that clothing be passed down from one sibling to another. These natural-occurring circumstances created the perfect foil for graffiti writers in this emerging subculture, where a baggy hooded sweatshirt could be used to hide your identity when illegally "tagging" property. It also helped early breakdancers ease the friction on the surfaces of the original cardboard box when they were doing a headspin or a windmill.

Given their limited access to traditional means of social mobility, jewelry accessories have always been a symbol of power for these youth, saying to a world that devalues black communities that "I am a somebody." During hip hop's first phase of influence in the early 1980s, jewelry accessories like large Liberace-esque chains and gold necklaces were worn as symbols of perceived wealth and to demonstrate that black people are descendants of African kings and queens, not the 'hood dwellers that Fox News makes them out to be. During the black nationalism era of the 1990s, a dizzying number of rap aliases carried queen and king titles (e.g., Queen Latifah, King Sun), trading in their gold chains for pendants with Africa continent medallions, and flip flopping Adidas gear for Kenyan kente cloth-inspired creations.[5]

Much like producers sampling music to create new

beat structures, the same effect happens when rappers appropriate clothing staples from Ralph Lauren or high quality Timberland boots. Every hip hop scene around the world puts its own unique twist on styles invented by American youth.

Outside of the US, hip hoppers from Burma to Bangladesh absorb largely Western rap styles — wearing the same G-Unit T-shirts and dollar sign jewelry pendants — due to widespread exposure to American culture via satellite television and the World Wide Web. Sadly, these media imperialists tend to project images of mostly male artists wearing oversized clothes, without explaining the context. Women within the culture are found wearing the opposite — either extremely tight clothes or they are scantily clad. Both types of objectification are more a product of global patriarchy and sexism than being directly tied to hip hop. Hip hop did not invent the idea of the half-dressed female, but sadly it is now a great disseminator of such values.

Different cultures adapt hip hop fashion to their own regional traditions and twists. Established African rappers like Ugandan Bataka Squad or Senegalese Daara J are wearing African motifs, headwraps or textiles interwoven or draped onto traditional baggy clothes pieces. In any kingdom where the Qur'an serves as the constitution, such as Saudi Arabia, the struggle with the effects of intrusive Western-style modernity are more marked. If women must cover their hair and wear a cloak in public, no amount of Phat Farm clothing advertisements in glossy magazines will do anything to change that.

Japanese Appropriation

Nowhere was hip hop fashion appropriation more marked than in Japan in the 1990s. American hip hop music has been popular there since the screening of the seminal hip hop film *Wild Style* in 1983, but many of the Japanese fans did not speak English and so did not understand what the rappers were saying. This may explain why the Japanese scene seems more focused on the look of hip hop than on its message.[6]

Acting and looking like an African American hip hopper is one of the most important facets of the Japanese scene. However, some Japanese hip hop fans misinterpreted hip hop's message of inclusiveness and thought that being a hip hop fan meant that you needed to literally look black. By the early 1990s, it was common for fans to go to tanning salons or use products to darken their skin (one such product was called African Special).[7] Many fans and performers wear hooded sweatshirts and their hair in dreadlocks or have it puffed into Afros. Some Japanese artists even paint their faces black. If you were to ask genuine Afro-wearing hip hoppers about other cultural groups mimicking their cultural stylings, you would find occasional feelings of resentment. After all, they're wearing the cloak of "authentic" black cultural behavior without having to deal with the implications of being black and male in the US and around the world. Non-black rap fans need to consider more creative ways of paying homage to this rich African culture than resorting to full-blown cultural appropriation.

Chapter 5
Hip Hop Herstory and Pride Rap

She Got Game

Women have been involved in hip hop from the beginning — from Sha Rock's lyrical contribution to the seminal 1979 rap song "That's the Joint" by the Funky Four + One More to Sylvia Rhone, who controlled Sugar Hill Records, which released rap's first pop crossover hit "Rapper's Delight." Sugar Hill also signed Sequence, the first all-female emcee crew to release a record in the mid-1980s.

Why have women's stories become obscure, rarely mentioned footnotes in rap lore? And why do rap temptresses like Jacki-O, Trina and Lil' Kim get all the glory? The answer is quite simple, and it starts with an "s." The same sexism that plagues society at large is what's helped transform some of rap's most genuine ovaried talents into sexpots who figure it's the only way their voices might get heard alongside those of their largely male rap counterparts.

The re-telling of hip hop histories that omit crucial female contributions begins early with the story of rap's

New York genesis. Most hip hop culture accounts that mention Kool Herc — rap's acknowledged founding father — and his early innovations rarely, if ever, mention hip hop's first solo female emcee, Pebblee Poo, who was so talented that she got recruited to rhyme alongside Herc's pioneering Herculoids sound system.

By 1984, Roxanne Shanté's "Roxanne's Revenge," a response record made to tackle the overt sexism in rap group UTFO's song, "Roxanne Roxanne," sold half a million records. In 1989, hip hoppers were privy to Queen Latifah's hit song "Ladies First," which listed the accomplishments of women, and in the early 1990s, "U.N.I.T.Y.," a collaborative song with fellow female emcee Monie Love, which spoke out against men disrespecting women: "instinct brings me to another flow/every time I hear a brotha call a girl a bitch or a ho." Salt-N-Pepa took things further as the first female act to land a gold record with *Very Necessary*.

By the mid to late 1990s, there appeared to be a major breakthrough, as Lil' Kim, Foxy Brown, Lauryn Hill, Missy Elliott and Eve all received widespread acknowledgment in the areas of record sales (Kim and Brown had multi-platinum sales of their respective debuts), awards (Hill's *Miseducation* was the first hip hop album to win Album of the Year at the Grammys) and chart toppings (Eve's *Ruff Ryders' First Lady* debuted at number one on the *Billboard* 200).

Sadly, today these same female voices are scant to nonexistent. In 2004, the Recording Academy nixed the best female rap artist category due to a shortage of eligible entries. The only area in which femcees have kept pace with their rap brothers is in the area of crime and incarceration, with these same attention-grabbing, award-winning rappers Lil' Kim, Foxy Brown, Remy Ma and Da Brat all serving jail time for offenses ranging from perjury to assault and manslaughter. Then there's the case of Lauryn Hill, who seems to have fallen victim to mental health issues in the face of her success.

Why has the clock on equality been turned back? In a music genre where women are a target of male rappers' lyrics, and misogyny and objectification are pretty much de rigueur, a lot has changed in just two decades. When Sha Rock introduced rap fans to an atypical gendered rap outlook and voice in the 1970s, women in hip hop traveled the rap map.

Teremoana Rapley, the first female rapper in New Zealand, cut her teeth performing as a teenager with Upper Hutt Posse, arguably the country's first respected rap crew, in the 1980s. She explained to me in a 2009 online interview that the gender divide in her country is not too wide.

"We (females) get the same sort of treatment, usually respect for our skills in this art form," she says. She admits that being a self-described "tomboy" meant that the "majority of the chauvinistic attitudes were left at the door." She believes that for women to be taken seriously in hip hop, they need to work behind the scenes and control their own image, and not rely on men to produce their music or shoot their videos.

"In a board room…this is where the real chauvinism

rears its ugly head…most of their (record label) ideas are based on our looks and their interpretation of what a female emcee should be, not what I am or my skills.

"I have acknowledged the challenge and developed the necessary skills to take into combat. I learned to develop websites, computer graphics…I have been using recording equipment since the late 1980s, and I write, direct, shoot, present and produce television and therefore music videos and documentaries."

Yet if you were to scan American TV, the role of women has been relegated to video dancer and mere accomplice sideshow, or women are treated as a novelty act, like a white rapper in an overwhelmingly black male-dominated form. Nowhere is this more evident than on schmaltzy American reality TV shows like VH1's *Salt-N-Pepa* or *Miss Rap Supreme*, where female rap contestants based in the "Fembassy" are satirically asked to cross-dress to appear like their famous male counterparts or perform seductive rap songs in lesbian bars.

Detroit rapper Invincible, who recorded one of the best female rap debuts in over a decade — *ShapeShifters* — is obscure. Her being Caucasian provokes suspicions that she is part of some post-Feminem calling (she actually rejected a $1 million record label deal during Eminem's tenure to avoid comparisons). She's a lesbian and a Palestinian sympathizer who happens to be an Israeli-born Jew, meaning other cards are stacked against her.

A large chunk of the rap videos that rotate on BET and MTV flaunt scantily clad "video hotties," while male rappers such as Nelly openly treat female bodies badly on screen. For example, Nelly's controversial "Tip Drill" video includes a scene where a credit card is swiped down a woman's bum.[1] No matter what Nelly raps about, his videos eventually come back to urging women in successively creepy ways to take off their clothes. Nelly has a great voice and great abs — what he doesn't have is a clue. Even Stevie Wonder can see that his videos are dreadful.

The use of sexually suggestive images to sell just about everything, including rap music, means consumers owe it to themselves to go a bit deeper on the issue. Sure, misogyny is deeply rooted in the cultures in which we live, and hip hop is an easy target because it's largely produced by downtrodden racialized group members. But where's the accountability and personal responsibility from the artists themselves? Or from the record labels who fund these irresponsible projects, and the video networks who rotate these offensive videos ad nauseam?

It's not enough for rap apologists to blame society without turning the lens on themselves as active participants in this chronic perpetuation of sexism, and without aggressively seeking out corrective measures. Why? Because hip hop is the leading voice of youth culture. Its particular embrace of misogynistic lyrical content and Tip Drill-styled imagery is hazardous to everyone's health.

While rap's treatment of women has hit a low point, sexist themes were always present in old-school rap. What we should question is why this imagery continues to be so pervasive in the culture today.

Outernational Women's Rap

Female emcees outside of the US have arguably played a much larger role in the history and development of the genre. The Sri Lankan and England bred femcee M.I.A. is the current torchbearer. Her raps have so penetrated the global rap scene that male American emcees are sampling and covering her songs. "Swagga Like Us," which samples M.I.A.'s voice, excerpted from her *Paper Planes* hit, was re-recorded by four of America's premier rap talents — Jay-Z, T.I., Kanye West and Lil Wayne in 2008.

In Canada, Michie Mee was the first Canadian emcee, regardless of gender, to be signed to an American major label deal (First Priority, 1988). In the UK, Monie Love was arguably the first rapper to break the British rap presence out of its non-threatening international rap designation. Her rhymes were dope, she just happened to be a female, and she received genuine respect from real hip hoppers for her work with Native Tongues and Queen Latifah.

Ms. Dynamite is one of only two rapper/R&B acts to win the Mercury Prize (given to the most outstanding musician in England and Ireland) since its inception in 1992. Likewise, UK's Lady Sovereign stands out in the Grime scene, an offshoot rap subgenre that blends dancehall, UK garage and rap. Signed to a lucrative recording contract by rapper Jay-Z in 2005, many argue she's just another white artist who's been prematurely elevated in her career due to the Feminem phenomenon — major labels scooping up white female emcees in the hope of scoring another breakout international white rap success story. Her middling 2009 *Jigsaw* release has done nothing to prove otherwise.

And in Morocco, where hip hop's influence is being strongly felt, a crew of women placed first in Ouf du Bled, the country's first hip hop competition held in Casablanca in 2008.[2]

The sexism and misogyny expressed in commercial rap song lyrics and video imagery that dominate the charts in North America might be outright banned elsewhere. In Cuba, for example, the women's rap movement was largely founded on challenging the machismo inherent in the culture and the wider patriarchy. Cuban hip hop has had an enormous impact on the global rap scene, especially in terms of the participation of women. The state-supported rap agency is run by a woman (Magia, one-half of Obsesion, the most popular Cuban rap group). DJ Leydis, now based in California, has helped develop a strong feminist presence by co-founding Omega Kilay, an all-women collective composed of Cuban deejays and rappers.

Cuban Telmary Díaz, originally from the group Free Hole Negro, is a vanguard in the women's rap movement. In a 2008 interview she told me that she sometimes gets viewed as sexually promiscuous — as do many black and mixed race women in the tourist economy — and the music gets ignored.

"The guys push the girls to be that way, to promote their sexuality, that's why I didn't match in that movement. What's important for me is the message, and I don't play that game. In Cuba, some guys look at it like competition. If they invite a woman on stage, it will take away some of the focus from them, and that's the challenge. At the same time, I try to be in the middle. I don't want to come off like a stereotypical tough hardcore rap guy. I love to keep my sensuality. But please focus on my content."

Telmary is inspired by American spoken-word artist Ursula Rucker, and works out of the tradition of Instincto, the island's first all-woman rap trio. She says, "They were a triple threat as far as female rap goes. One member was a great rapper, the other had a great voice, the other had sensuality. They inspired me." Telmary believes that the release of her solo debut, *A Diario*, and widespread exposure from tours outside the country have helped young female *raperas* begin to view hip hop as a legitimate way to express themselves and build a career.

"After hearing me front my own band, and release my own music, a lot of girls started to rap for themselves. All of the women who rap are behind the guys, they don't have their own space and career or their own band, and no one did it before. Cuba is a very macho society, and the rap scene reflects that, so when you see a woman like me commanding the stage, it's rare. Ten years ago, no one thought it would be possible. As a woman you are encouraged to think about other careers to make money and survive. Even when I first started with hip hop, my family didn't get it. They didn't consider it to be real music. All some people see is Buena Vista Social Club. But I found a way to mix hip hop with the classics from Los Van Van on my CD, and in that way eyes opened up.

I was defending my roots with my music, not trying to imitate another culture."

The Straight Jacket

It's fascinating that in the long, storied history of hip hop not one single successful or mainstream rapper, producer, breakdancer, graffiti writer, deejay, beat boxer or turntablist has come out of the closet. Not one. Zero. Nada.

While there is a burgeoning underground LGBT (lesbian, gay, bisexual, transsexual) scene, which has featured veterans from Tori Fixx to DEADLEE, and a newer school of groups like Yo Majesty, whose electro rap concoctions have led to tour opportunities alongside Brazilian baile punk mavens CSS (Cansei de Ser Sexy – I Got Tired of Being Sexy), these musicians largely play to an insider audience of LGBT fans. The world of the homosexual hip hopper has limited options outside of the obvious subcultural support networks.

Other music genres don't have the same story to tell. In country and western we know of Canada's k.d. lang, rock'n'roll's Freddie Mercury (Queen) or Elton John, pop music's Lance Bass (*NSYNC) or George Michael, jazz's Dave Koz, house music's Frankie Knuckles or Larry Levan, R&B's Luther Vandross — and the list goes on and on. It's nearly the second decade of the twenty-first century and anything should be possible. The best golfer in the world is black. America has a black president. So why not a gay platinum rapper?

If rap is considered underground music, the world of

the gay rapper is below water. One view of this within black communities is that there is a double standard for white musicians, who come out of the closet and get widespread support. But if you're black and you come out, your career is jeopardized. And rappers have enough fatwas out on them already from conservative middle white America, so coming out as a rapper is not the wisest career move.

Is hip hop the last bastion of heterosexuality in the music industry? And does LGBT living exist on a separate island from hip hop? It's highly unlikely that of the hundreds of rap releases annually since the 1980s Golden Era, none of the rappers is transgendered, gay or lesbian. The law of averages makes it virtually impossible, considering that statistics or long-running urban legends estimate that one out of every ten people is gay.

Hip hop has convicted murderers (C-Murder), declared pimps (Too Short, Gorgeous Dre, Bishop Don "Magic" Juan), former gang members (the late Eazy-E), drug dealers (Jay-Z), porn stars (Heather Hunter) and doctors (Roxanne Shanté). But gays or lesbians? Hardly. Homosexuality is hip hop's last taboo. This is ironic considering that the rap genre, arguably more than any other, prides itself on its ability to depict injustice, speak untold truths, expose the underexposed, be a voice to the voiceless. As the oldest known rap catchphrase insists, the culture's genuine practitioners "keep it real." On one hand you have a rap community that's always being victimized and discriminated against for race, dress codes and subject matter. Yet on the other hand this community continues to discriminate against and persecute another community in its lyrics.

Why is rap music one of the few music forms that openly assaults gay community members with impunity? The answer may lie in hip hop's roots in street culture, where over-the-top machismo drove the music's earliest energies. Much as in the hyper macho world of athletics, it's a faux pas even to suggest that a male is effeminate. Grandmaster Flash's "The Message," one of the genre's seminal anthems about street culture, refers to "sissies."

Gay stereotypes run counter to the bravado and posturing necessary to gain credibility in rap. Some of rap's biggest stars and sellers, including Eminem, DMX and Ice Cube have used blatantly homophobic lyrics. On Eminem's "Criminal" he raps: "Whether you're a fag or a lez, or the homo sex, hermaph, or a trans-a-vest, pants or dress — hate fags? The answer's yes."

Others, like rapper Trick Trick from Detroit, made famous for his collaborations with Eminem, hurled vicious lyrical assaults at gay activists like Rosie O'Donnell and Ellen DeGeneres on his 2008 debut, *The Villain* (he refers to them as "dyke bitches" on the album's self-titled track).[3] Trick Trick is a little-known underground rapper, so his lyrics and music don't hit mass audiences. But critics wonder if Eminem were black instead of white whether he would have experienced the type of concert bans or backlash treatment that A-list reggae artists routinely get.

Given the homophobia and machismo that exist in Cuba, a unique aspect of the local rap scene is that the openly lesbian rap group Las Krudas Cubensi continues to speak out against gender imbalance and homophobia, both on and off the island. Formed in 2000, Las Krudas Cubensi took part in the Pop Montreal Festival (2005) and the Queer Music Festival in Tennessee in 2006. Their widely circulated underground debut release *Krudas Cubensi* (2002) is a trail-blazing marker in support of the rights of Cuban queer communities.[4]

The most influential rapper of the new millennium, Kanye West, shed some light on hip hop and the broader society's uneasy relationship with LGBT communities. On the August 22, 2005, MTV special *All Eyes on Kanye*, he equated the civil rights struggles of African Americans with those of gays and acknowledged that "everyone in hip hop discriminates against gay people." An inaccurate overgeneralization, but it made the point. West's epiphany came when he learned his cousin was gay. "I love him and I've been discriminating against gays." He's not exactly afraid to speak his mind or express his vulnerable side (he slammed ex-president George Bush in a post-Hurricane Katrina rant in front of a nationally televised audience of twenty million, saying, "George Bush does not like black people"). But just to demonstrate the Cheech and Chong-high level of distaste of gay constituencies in rap circles, West later said that his "standing up for gays was even more crazy than bad-mouthing the president."[5]

Pride Rap Resource

A burgeoning movement of gay and lesbian American rappers perform under the "Homo Hop" umbrella movement.

Pick Up the Mic: The 2005 documentary takes us into the queer rap underworld. It is the pop culture item that brought this largely underground rap scene to the attention of the wider society.

The HomoRevolution Tour: In 2007, the first Homo Hop tour in LGBT history was limited to swing dates in the Southwest US, largely considered a gay-friendly region. In 2008, the Hard Gay tour mimicked HomoRevolution's energies but was restricted to California.

OutHipHop.com: This website is the portal and virtual meeting place for LGBT rappers.

Hiding in Hip Hop: This book penned by Terrance Dean describes a "down-low" existence, a world where black males who consider themselves straight sleep with other men. But in its 320 pages, it doesn't out anybody either.

Chapter 6
Rap's Social Conscience

The North American rap scene is not one big, phat, homogenous one-trick capitalist pony, as it's portrayed on Black Entertainment Television. There are as many rappers interested in environmental issues and addressing the 'isms (race, sex, class) and schisms that plague Western societies as there are interested in teaching you how to cut up crack cocaine and operate prostitution rings. Just because MTV doesn't play it doesn't mean it's not relevant or isn't being produced or celebrated. We can all thank Jah for blessing the world with YouTube, a broadcast portal for "the people," where videos created with no budget can generate the same global impact and audience as something shown on MuchMusic.

Many of the most poignant raps in the history of the music form are less about bling and more about the beautification of inner-city streets. If consumers or rap purists are looking for a more genuine articulation of rap's modus operandi, they need look no further than the artistic output of wordsmiths dubbed "Conscious Rappers." Though many of these issues-oriented rappers themselves loathe the title and pigeonholing process that comes with fans expecting their every move and verbal articulation to be socially responsible, these wordsmiths work out of the tradition of what rap was created for — to be a voice for voiceless racialized groups, and to speak out on pertinent social issues.

A few key figures helped popularize the concept of marrying good art with commerce *and* social awareness — a difficult task to pull off in Western capitalist societies, where generating cash is the be-all and end-all. KRS-One, rap's most prolific emcee, who's had over twenty full-length releases to his name, founded the Stop the Violence movement in 1989, a campaign to address violence in the black community through education, grassroots organizing and direct action.[1]

Raptivist functions were further propelled by Public Enemy, who emerged during rap's Black Conscious era (1987-1993), a time when the children of 1960s civil rights supporters were feeling a turning back of the social and political gains of their parents' generation and needed to re-articulate the voice of oppressed communities.

This rap movement acted as a backlash against the stench left by the congressional hearings led by Tipper Gore (wife of former presidential candidate Al). The campaign created Parental Advisory stickers, viewed as a direct attack against rappers who spoke harsh truths on celluloid. And there was no black leader like Barack Obama who was tapped into youth concerns or could speak to the multiplicity of issues that plagued this generation. Self-appointed community leaders like the

Reverends Jesse Jackson and Al Sharpton, while respected, were viewed as out-of-touch old-school mouthpieces
of a generation's past.

As a musical ensemble, Public Enemy managed to
gather wide appeal, generate large revenues, sound funky
and at the same time drive home salient political agendas
and points. For example, "Fight the Power," a protest
anthem featured on filmmaker Spike Lee's *Do the Right
Thing*, implores people to fight for their human rights
over a funky bass line, while dissing iconic American
actor John Wayne for what he was — an unrepentant
racist and white supremacist.[2]

New School Raptivism

There's a whole new current crop of emcees who aren't
afraid to call the kettle black, or The Man wack (not
good). Many of them emerged in the 1990s, including
Common (who supported America's first black president,
Barack Obama, in his song "The People" a full year
before his presidency); Mos Def (who's attached himself
to many social causes, including the restoration of New
Orleans following Hurricane Katrina, attacking the US
government's glacially slow response); Peruvian rapper
Immortal Technique (arguably the most underrated raptivist, who's sold more than 135,000 units without the
aid of a major label); and the Coup (who almost had
their 2001 *Party Music* album permanently shelved for
including an image of the World Trade Center being
blown up months before it actually did on 9/11).[3]

In North America, the group with the most grassroots

currency and resonance is the hyper-political duo of Dead Prez, who have devoted their lives and careers to erasing the legacy of slavery, Jim Crow and Bush administration blunders. Not only have they recorded one of rap's most poignant protest songs of all time, "Hip Hop," they've created an RBG (Revolutionary But Gangsta) movement that funnels their underground rap releases onto the streets where their voices matter. They coordinate an annual Black August benefit concert in NYC and Cuba to raise funds in defense of imprisoned American Black Panther civil rights-era freedom fighters like Romaine "Chip" Fitzgerald, who many activists argue was falsely convicted for a police shooting. Or like Assata Shakur, also alleged to have taken part in police shootings in the early 1970s, who's been forced to live in exile. Shakur's story in particular has captured the imagination of the hip hop generation for her outlaw maverick status and pure bravery in the face of stiff government opposition. Shakur escaped from a women's prison in New Jersey in 1979 and subsequently fled to Cuba, where she was granted political asylum by Fidel Castro and has been living since 1984. A who's who of politically aware contemporary rap talents, including Common, Dead Prez and Mos Def, have either recorded tributes to her or actively speak out in her defense, specifically regarding the $1 million bounty placed on her head by the FBI.[4]

The irony and running joke in Black Conscious rap circles is that these highly politicized anti-establishment rap acts usually attract more white audiences than black. While there's no research on concert demographic data, people in the scene, including performers and promoters, estimate that between 85 and 95 percent of the people at Conscious Rap concerts are white.[5]

Outside of the West, there are raptivist heavyweight figures like Sudanese-bred, London-based Emmanuel Jal, who uses his rhymes to illuminate issues in his home country. For Jal, a former child soldier who at the age of nine was an active member of the Sudan People's Liberation Army, rap music and activism are inextricably linked. During a 2009 interview in Toronto, he told me about the atrocities he's witnessed and been a part of and spoke movingly about hip hop's potential for healing communities.

"In Africa, it (hip hop) is the news outlet about what is happening. And it's the only thing that speaks to our mind, heart, soul…every word that an emcee spits, you see a picture, and it comes out of urgency. Emcees are our emotional leaders. If you go to a place that's suffering, that's what you'll hear."

Jal takes particular offense at Western-based rappers who underestimate how their rhymes about gunplay, buying jewelry and scoring hot women can indoctrinate African youth. "My cousin stabbed a white boy. He's a refugee in the UK. Why? Because he wanted to be a gangsta like 50 Cent."

On his 2009 CD *Warchild*, a song titled "50 Cent" challenges the iconic New York-based rapper to clean up his image and stop promoting violence. In his early years, 50 Cent became newsworthy, not so much for his rhyme skills, but for the fact that he got shot nine times in 2000 and survived, and for recording lurid fantasies about robbing his fellow rappers on "How to Rob," his first buzzworthy song.

"Go to Africa, and he's the icon of the music, and a lot of kids worship him," explains Jal, whose autobiography, also titled *War Child*, is one of the most profound reads in the Western "child soldier" publishing cottage industry. "But the disadvantage is, they think it's cool to be a gangsta, it's cool to kill. So every kid is arming themselves. You go to a club, you step on someone's shoes, and they want to chuck a knife at you. Drop out of school to get rich quick or die trying." (*Get Rich or Die Trying* is the name of 50 Cent's debut album.)

"I may never get a chance to call 50 Cent on the phone, but let me pass my message, what I want to say through music. Whether he likes it or not, somehow he'll hear it. If he replies to it, that's up to him. But at least he got what I'm telling him. It's not dissing him, it's giving him his respect — but to point out to him that in places where people are happy and there's no issues, they can talk about Mercedes-Benz, guns and women. I come from a place where we have a lot of issues, so I can't talk about ladies. I have to talk about rescuing kids from war. About healing black communities. Kids don't know you only die once."

Despite the hope that hip hop provides for Jal, he admits that it's not that simple. No great rhyme concoction can cure him of all that ails his mind when he reflects that he had a hand in killing Muslims because he was programmed as a child soldier to do so. "Sometimes the wounds that are healed get scratched. There's my sister's pain — she got raped several times in the war. When I watch TV and I see the situation in Darfur, I put my frustration in the music, and it becomes therapy."

Religion and Rap

Journalist "The Media Assassin" Harry Allen describes Islam as hip hop's "official religion." Certainly many of American rap's most important contemporary and politically astute voices claim to be devout Muslims. They include Freeway, Rakim, Common, K'naan, Mos Def and Lupe Fiasco — taking their lead from hip hop pioneer Afrika Bambaataa.

Grammy-winning group Public Enemy and its charismatic front man, Chuck D, carried on this tradition in the 1990s by sampling fiery Nation of Islam black power leader Louis Farrakhan in its music. The Nation of Islam, Five Percent Nation and Sunni Muslims all have differences among their communities and in their style of worship, but all acknowledge the transformative power of the Qur'an.

How did these communities of hip hop and Islam become compatible in the West? One could argue that both are vast transglobal transformative cultural movements with a strong protest ethic and the sense of being under attack by Western morality gauges. One is the fastest growing religious culture in the world, the other the fastest growing youth culture music form, and both are unrestricted in terms of race, gender, age and geography.

However, in Saudi Arabia, home to Islam's holiest places, Mecca and Medina, where religious sensibilities and moral codes are strong, the compatibility between the Muslim religion and rap is not as rosy as it might be in the West.

In fact, rap, which carries X-rated lyrics and negative female video imagery, is generally not well received in a city where concerts are often banned, where there are no nightclubs due to social and religious codes, where alcohol is banned, and where the popular Western dating rituals of unrelated men and women hooking up for good times is frowned upon.

When members of the popular Saudi hip hop group Dark2Men placed well in a 2008 MTV Arabia competition, it was after years of hiding their professional hobby from relatives who view hip hop rhymes and dance styles as decadent, and opposed to Islam.

"There are a lot of Saudi rappers, but they're underground because of the wrong impression people have of them," says group leader Mansour, recounting how his father, a retired school principal, threatened to disown him a day after their rap video clip aired on MTV. Fellow group member Zain says their major challenge is to make their family and peers understand that they are as serious about their religion and their culture as they are about hip hop. "People don't understand us here. They think being part of a rap group means you're less Arab or less Muslim or you want to imitate the West."[6] Certainly American rap personalities like DJ Khaled or Swizz Beatz, who practice the Muslim faith and simultaneously utter many profanities in their music, do little to quell the fears of devout Muslims.

In France, most of the rap artists or groups of note like IAM happen to be Muslims of North African descent, so Muslim ideologies figure prominently in their lyrics. While other major world religions like Christianity carry large offshoot subgenres like Gospel Rap, their rap personalities and successes have not penetrated secular audiences inside or outside of the US.

Cuba's New Revolución

In Cuba, the rap revolution embraces the local political situations of the day — the two are inseparable. Given the socialist economy, making big money and sporting nugget-sized jewelry has never been a part of any equation. It's not about making a profit; it's about making a difference. Rap is employed as an activity to keep youth off the streets and away from the lure of violence or illegal activity. Unlike in the US, it gets little or no fiscal support from corporations or sponsors. In fact, most high-profile Cuban rappers have strong ties to black power movements that are consumed with human rights issues and political resistance, a far cry from their American counterparts' relationships with big business.

As rap music hit an early apex in the 1990s in the West, an interesting phenomenon was happening during Cuba's economic crisis. In Havana, restrictions on foreign content were relaxed on the country's rudimentary radio and TV antennas. As English language signals reached Cuban shores, the tales of disenfranchised black communities hit home in a country where blacks of African descent make up over 70 percent of the population.[7] Despite the language barrier, burgeoning Cuban artists aligned with Black Power movements related to this feeling of being second-class citizens in their home country. Cuba endured some of the worst aspects of the slave trade and the genocide of its indigenous people before that. The manifestations of these legacies are evident in the underemployment of blacks, especially in the key tourist industry, the source of much-needed foreign currency. One feature of Fidel Castro's revolution that has worked, and is not open to debate, is the increased social mobility that blacks have enjoyed since 1959. However, racism has not been eliminated under socialism. Afro-Cubans are a little better off than they were before the revolution, but it might take a new generation of rappers to address this topic publicly.

Today, Cuban rap is refreshingly issues-oriented and linked to struggle, much like early New York City rap — before the Benzes, bling and booty fixations. And as is the case with hip hop in most places around the globe, Cubans take hip hop and make it their own, sampling indigenous Cuban salsa and rhumba. At the annual Festival de Rap Cubano in Alamar, east Havana, started in 1995, organizers have forged links between politicized rappers throughout the African diaspora, including American trailblazers Dead Prez, Mos Def, Common and The Roots.

The irony is that rap is rarely broadcast on Cuban radio or TV, and is relegated to suppressed underground culture status, despite its grip on the overall society. Some of the more popular groups in the Cuban hip hop diaspora, including Obsesion, Doble Filo or Free Hole Negro, don't live on the island anymore. Much of their success and reach is limited, because few Cuban groups who left are still heard on the island, and the material gains of those who take up the rap profession are few and far between. The first group to achieve international success was the Orishas, now based in France.

The Cuban government's support for the arts and the preservation of culture led to the creation of a Cuban Rap Agency in 2002. No other country in the world has a state-supported hip hop agency.[8] The agency's work falls in line with Cuba's other cultural institutions. The *casa cultura* in most neighborhoods supplies dated but functional music recording equipment, and fosters bottom-up art projects. However, critics see the agency as simply a tool of surveillance to guard against youth rappers critical of government policies and to curb any potential for protest.

As one rapper told me, "Rappers in Cuba are street journalists because the newspapers aren't talking about what is really happening; we don't have press freedoms, democracy. We don't have a salsa agency or a rock or folk agency. And then there is a rap agency? They just want to control us. In our lyrics we talk about how they don't recognize hip hop as true art; how we don't have possibilities to travel outside the country and uplift our careers in a major way. So I never wanted to be a part of the rap agency."[9]

Hip hop has never had any rules or any official global

governing body (the Zulu Nation acts more as an international hip hop awareness body, and its influence has diminished greatly over time). The mere idea of any state government, regardless of political ideology (socialism, capitalism, communism), supporting an outlaw music and culture invented to speak out against oppression in all its forms is oxymoronic at the least, contradictory at the best. But then again, ex-Cuban president Fidel Castro (and his brother Raúl, who took over in 2006) has always marched to his own beat, his views flying in the face of the West.

The influence of the Reggaeton genre, blending Jamaican rhythms with hip hop-fuelled Latin American rhyme styles, is diminishing the lure of the more social issues-oriented rap, as it features a seductive blend of American-styled capitalistic trends and exploits geared toward sex, scantily clad women, money fixations and crime.

Voice of the Banlieues

The largest rap scene outside of the US lies in France. Boasting many platinum rappers from MC Solaar to IAM, the rap landscape has always bubbled with a healthy mix of art and commerce. As in the US and the UK, where lazy bureaucrats have blamed hip hop for everything from teen pregnancy to drug addiction,[10] this scene is considered to be a threat. In late 2005, there were violent clashes between youth and authorities in the *banlieues* (suburban slums) of Paris after two youths hiding from police were accidentally electrocuted.

French rappers were blamed for inciting youth to riot with anti-government lyrics.

The stark reality had nothing to do with rap music. The riots were viewed more as an expression of frustration from the mostly North African black and Arab migrant youth due to high unemployment, lack of opportunity, police harassment and racism. Unemployment of youth between 18 and 25 years nears 40 percent in those parts of town, significantly higher than the national average of 8 percent.[11]

Racism within French society plays a large role in the success of French hip hop. Many French rappers are products of the HLM (*habitation à loyer modéré*) or subsidized housing, where France's heaviest concentration of North and West African immigrants use their tough upbringings as sources of inspiration for their lyrics.

After the riots, which made international headlines, 152 conservatives in the French parliament brought a lawsuit against seven rap groups for fostering hatred and racism against whites and for what one politician called "anti-French" sentiments.[12]

The unsuccessful legal action taken against them is part of the government war of attrition against hip hop. Yet Pierre, the eldest son of French president Nicolas Sarkozy — who referred to suburban youth as "scum" while interior minister in 2005 — has been "outed" as a hip hop producer, going by a pen name to avoid being linked to his father. Pierre Sarkozy produced beats for Parisian rapper Poison, who is a fierce critic of the French president.[13]

Chapter 7
The Globalization of Hip Hop

Hip hop is the leading global youth subculture. Despite being spread out over seven continents and performing amidst conflict and corruption in dozens of countries, practitioners consider themselves to be a part of one clique. Race, religion, geography, class, gender and age distinctions become less important as rap aficionados take Western hip hop skills and influence and transform them to fit their own society's needs.

In China, for example, age is not as huge a factor in hip hop's growing popularity as it is in the US. A group called the Hip Hop Grannies, a thirty-member all female group of sixty-year-old plus retirees, perform hip hop dance routines both for entertainment and high-energy exercise. They're performing on tour and taking China by storm. Group leader Wu became interested after watching hip hop-themed youth shows and fashion on TV, including the first National Hip Hop Dancing Competition on Chinese television in 2003.[1]

On the generational flipside, two child turntablists under the age of ten from Osaka, Japan, the sister-brother DJ duo Sara and Ryusei, are becoming two of the most talked about DJs on the planet, mostly for their raw technique and skill.[2] They already sport sponsorship deals from Vestax – the world's leading supplier of turntable equipment – after having entered an online Unknown DJ battle and generating over a million views on YouTube.

Due to hip hop's adaptability across nations, rap can be considered the new "world music," an offensive but still widely used term that lumps all non-Western musics from Cuban salsa to Israeli klezmer into one shapeless category. Why? Because the modern-day global rap explosion involves musicians from around the globe putting their own cultural twist on the *same* genre of music, so if any music form might be considered a "world music," it's rap.

Bollywood Beatz

Hip hop has mostly been a tale of Western rap styles colonizing the rest of the world, but South Asian classical music scenes and the first-generation children of Indian immigrants in the US, UK and Canada have begun to illustrate how cultural influence can flow from East to West as well. Many North American hip hoppers heard the linkages between American rap and South Asia when Jay-Z collaborated with Panjabi MC on a remix version of "Beware of the Boys" in 2004. From a sonic standpoint the East-West divide had already been bridged both ways, with Timbaland's tabla samples on Missy Elliott's "Get Ur Freak On" (2001), while Delhi-born DJ

Bally Sagoo had been blending classic Bollywood music with hip hop since the mid-1990s in England.[3]

Due to the unusually seamless blending of Punjabi bhangra beats created by dhol drums with traditional rap rhythms, other American producers like DJ Quik had hip hop fans looking to sitars for sonic inspiration. On Truth Hurts' "Addictive," he sampled Hindi artist Lata Mangeshkar. Unfortunately his record company, Aftermath, got sued for not getting clearance on the sample, and that might have deterred rap producers from recklessly plundering the vaults of Bollywood for beats.[4]

Others, like Snoop Dogg, have looked to broaden their appeal in an Indian market of over one billion residents, recording songs with legendary Indian rap trio RDB (Rhythm Dhol Bass) for use in Bollywood star Akshay Kumar's films.[5] But it's London-based rapper M.I.A. who has come up with a flawless formula to get global ears listening — fusing everything from electronic beats and Sri Lankan Tamil politics with hip hop swagger.

The African Way

The region arguably most affected by hip hop culture is Africa, in part due to its genetic linkages to the music (rappers fulfill the function of modern-day griots) and its historical interest in hip hop as the voice of voiceless diasporic black African people.

Popular Senegalese rapper Didier Awadi embodies these inherently Pan African hip hop connections. He, like many African rappers, including Daara J, got his inspiration from American rappers like Public Enemy, who used their art as a vehicle for activism. Some of his best works feature archival samples of speeches from iconic African political activist leaders such as Congo's Patrice Lumumba, in the same way Public Enemy samples civil rights leader Louis Farrakhan to circulate ideas on black community upliftment.

Didier, who raps mostly in French and Wolof (a language spoken in Senegal, the Gambia and Mauritania), says he does this to "get Africans to reappropriate their history." Didier says, "I take a speech by Kwame Nkrumah and mix it over a beat where I'm rapping, so it becomes a kind of intergenerational dialogue. Basically, I felt that we didn't know enough about our own history, our leaders, precisely at this time when there aren't enough real leaders."[6]

Rapper Composite K'naan

While the reach of most African rappers is limited to Africa and Europe, Somali rapper K'naan (Keinan Warsame) embodies the genuine face of rap's globalization, representing the first generation of youth from the continent taking Western rap forms and business savvy and fusing it with distinctly African musical traditions and interests. He's won over fans in both Africa *and* the West, a rare feat. Born and bred in Somalia, he represents a prototype of the globalized rapper of the future.

K'naan raps about Somalia, but in English. He's lived in Harlem, Toronto and Washington and has somehow been able to evade the pigeonholing process that plagues skilled African rappers like himself who aren't from hip hop's creative center, the US, and thus aren't given the same consideration for MTV play lists. His meteoric rise on both sides of the pond is unparalleled, generating accolades from "world music" constituents (2007 "Newcomer of the Year" by BBC Radio 3) and traditionalist Western raperati (2006 Juno Award — Canada's equivalent to the Grammy — for Best Rap Recording).

K'naan has recorded with many of the most important music voices, not just in the West, but throughout the Afro-diasporic music scenes, linking the griot-to-rap continuum much the way an ethnomusicologist would — from collaborations with Americans Mos Def and Dead Prez, to Senegalese and Mali superstars Youssou N'Dour and Amadou & Mariam, all the way to Jamaican reggae stalwarts Stephen and Damian Marley.

K'naan's music is a byproduct of the widespread emigration of Somalis fleeing civil war in the 1980s, and he's admitted to seeing more gun violence and tougher streets than your average gangster rapper. But rather than glorifying violence for increased CD sales, he uses these histories to create an unrepentant, new-world-styled protest music, as evidenced on his first global hit song, "Soobax."

"It's more than a song; it's something people raise arms for," he told me in a 2004 interview.[7] Recorded over a cavalcade of muffled percussion sounds, the audio is mixed together to convey confrontational emotions. "Soobax" means "come out with it" — that is, let the warlords and gunmen know that you've had enough of it. Partly in English, with the catchy hook recorded in his native tongue, K'naan directly challenges Somali war-lords:

> Dadkii waa dhibtee nagala soobax
> (You have exasperated the people so come out with it)
> Dhiigi waad qubtee nagala soobax
> (You've spilled the blood so that it drains on the
>   Roads, so come out with it)

> Hear me though, I work for the struggle I don't work
> For dough, I mean what I say, I don't do it for show,
> Somalia needs all gunmen right out the door.[8]

K'naan goes even deeper on his 2009 album *Troubadour*, addressing touchy topics, from Somali sea pirates to what it's like to fire a gun at the age of eight. His rap writing style, which is an assault on complacency and all that can be perceived as warm and fuzzy, is fully intentional. K'naan explains: "When I recorded that ("Soobax") in the studio, I imagined myself being in front of gunmen, and I'm communicating directly to them. When my brother heard the song he said that it's the first song he'd heard of mine that could get me killed." He adds: "My long-term goal is to use whatever music I present, or whatever fame for political purposes, to bring attention to, and change the situation in my region."[9] Longtime music critics like myself have many reasons to believe he can change the face of the music — and the world that surrounds it.

Portuguese Rap Styles

In Portugal, where fado music reigns supreme, Sam the Kid emerged as one of the most significant musical voices in 2001, kick-starting Portuguese hip hop. Influenced by American underground old-school rap icons like Souls of Mischief, Sam the Kid's music is renowned for its widespread and imaginative sampling. His debut recording, "Entre(tanto)," borrowed snippets from an array of media: homespun recordings, cassette tapes and video. His sophomore album, *Beats Vol. 1: Amor* — loosely based on his parents' romance — used a large archive of samples from an even wider palette of sound sources, including pornographic videos, telephone conversations and soap operas.

The second CD was voted one of the greatest Portuguese releases of the year. Despite his success Sam insisted to me in a 2008 interview that the Portuguese embrace of rap music is a work in progress. "I think it's considered a trend by some people but some others respect it as an art form. Rap music will never be as respected as fado because fado has roots in earlier ages, although there are some similarities. The public still sees us as worlds apart."

Sam is one of only a handful of Portuguese hip hoppers who can live modestly off his art. He admits that despite technological advances in the way musicians are able to transmit their music to global audiences via Internet circuits, finding listeners outside of Portugal is difficult. "Language is definitely one of the barriers, if not the only one," he said. He feels that "people can perceive the passion and truth of my work" even though they are unable to interpret his rhymes. "I think the Internet is a gift and a curse because it's easy for you to spread your music, but it's more difficult for you to stand out." As far as rap's ability to record and preserve local folk culture, from Sam's vantage point Portuguese hip hoppers reflect their own local concerns and cultures rather than reciting back stuff happening in America and abroad gleaned from MTV feeds. "We stay local subject-wise. Not many of us have a global kind of speech, and I think people here in Portugal connect with the lyrics exactly because of that."

With the ongoing threat of Western media imperialism, courtesy of vehicles like US-based CNN that is viewed in homes around the world, there is always the fear that the distinct local rap music in non-Western regions might fade out, or play second fiddle to what's hot in Atlanta. In many nations where rap reigns supreme amongst youth, there's a complex yet contradictory effect. As top-tier American rappers like Jay-Z continue to outsell and outshine indigenous artists in their own homelands, there is also a cultural reclamation process amongst rappers who want to redefine their distinct cultures and local identities for their own communities and for posterity.

Chapter 8
Black to the Future

Was Lil Wayne's ode to oral sexists, "Lollipop," really the best that rap humanity could come up with in 2008?[1] Many critics and rap fans young and old feel that listening to modern-day commercial rap is like having surgery without anesthesia. The chart-topping raps of Rick Ross and Soulja Boy are mostly inane and unsubstantial, and those over the age of twenty-five who bore witness to a brighter time, the Golden Era, are saying, "I want the 1980s back." For others it's still a new music, an acquired taste that was never considered real music to begin with, a passing trend like Rubik's Cubes and Chia pets.

We're all looking for some hip hope.

There are signs that rap's end could be near if its stakeholders don't act fast. The genre's most respected and impactful talents are mostly in their late thirties and early forties (e.g., Nas, Jay-Z, KRS-One, Mos Def), so where are their teenaged or twenty-something-year-old replacements? Certainly, when Nas, one of the top ten most influential rappers of all time, titles his eighth release *Hip Hop Is Dead*, and some of the culture's vanguards —

including Andre 3000 — rarely rap much now, saying the rap game is stale and needs rejuvenation, it's a problem. Is hip hop dead or dying? Is its carcass rotting, gutted by the marketing techniques of multinational corporations who are quick to hand out recording contracts to ex-drug dealers, but don't give the time of day to Green rappers interested in rhymes about reducing our carbon footprint? Has rap lost its direction? Does it need to be reborn? Has its cutting edge been dulled? Who's responsible for creating this bloated multinational company-sponsored monster, with a platinum-encrusted chain slung around its neck?

As Soulja Boy-styled hits continue to race up the charts, rap could end up on life support. But I want to hold on to it, shock it one more time with those electric paddles, give it that much-needed heart transplant and offer it some dialysis to clean out its system. Rap's progression from a rebellious and revolutionary art form to a commodity packaged by executives is not sitting well with many of its fans, including me. Political activism is now a too-small part of the hip hop nation, unlike in the 1980s when it was a dominant part.

Rap's original aim was to project youth angst by the bushel. But what happens when these angry young misfits are no longer so young or angry, when some of the more talented wordsmiths become wealthy and powerful and have nothing to whine about anymore? Can you still sing the blues when you're a multimillionaire? Don't we want our favorite artists to evolve, and not stay stuck in a time warp? Snoop Dogg is married and coaches his child's football team, so should he still be expected to create expletive-filled, vulgarity-laced verses about scoring a bunch of hot women and getting drunk nightly? Not during a time when America's first black president, Obama, officially endorsed by Snoop Dogg, inspires more optimism in global youth and less dwelling on the negative aspects of their daily lives.

And where's the originality? After the deaths by gunfire of two of the most prolific and proficient rappers of all time, Tupac Shakur and Notorious B.I.G., the Western rap marketplace has been stuck in a weird rut, with no sign that there will be any emcees capable of generating such a global impact. Tupac's posthumous CDs continue to outsell current releases, so what does that say about contemporary rap?[2]

Tragically Hip(ster) Rap

The electro- and hipster-inspired rap scene that took root in the mid-2000s is not so inspiring today, because it actually sounds like yesterday's rap. It's not expected to last long because it's essentially using the aesthetic of 1980s old-school rap. It is driven by fashion more than anything — patterned hoodies, high-top sneakers, form-fitted jeans and a laptop and presto — you're a rap hipster or is that hipster rapper? The true measures of what makes a great emcee (cadence, storytelling, voice, poetry rhymes, delivery, lyrics, creative use of literary devices) have been tossed aside in any discussion of hipster rap vanguards Spank Rock, Kid Sister, Peaches or Mickey Factz, whose collective rhyme skills might've gotten them the eggs-and-bottle-hurled-at-your-head treatment at Harlem's Apollo Theater.

There are signs that the hardcore street mantra and rhymes that defined rap's early moral center carry less sway with a hipster rap subculture. Some, who as children of middle-class parents benefiting from post-1970s civil rights gains, are part of a different narrative. We see this in the more emotionally based lyricism of neo-hipster, polyglot rappers K-OS from Canada or Cleveland's Kid Cudi, who could both be described as Emo Rap vanguards. Emo (short for emotional) Rap is a media-coined term used to describe rappers whose rhymes display some of the more vulnerable aspects of being a human being, and is a play on the Emo rock genre characterized by sensitive songwriting stylings. On Cudi's "Sky Might Fall," for example, he raps, "What a world that I'm livin' in/When do rainstorms ever end…Grey clouds up above mane/metaphor to my life mane." ("Mane" is man.)

The "hipster" concept is not exactly new. Norman Mailer's 1957 essay "The White Negro: Superficial Reflections on the Hipster" describes Caucasian youth who curiously co-opted many aspects of the black jazz movements from the 1920s to the 1940s. But many of the most important figures in the hipster rap scene, from Cool Kids to the Knux, are taking a retrospective musical approach, simply producing and rapping the way practitioners did in the early 1980s. This, combined with that flurry of derivative Futuro Hip Hop mash-up fusion sounds — from Ghettotronic to Grime or Ghetto Tech — has had a short shelf life. Is Hipster Rap dead? Did it ever stand a chance, given the diminished attention spans of its millennial music inventors?

Despite the apocalyptic doom and gloom scenarios being offered up on the state of rap music, a cornucopia of possibilities lies ahead. Like how about fusing country music and rap? Rap music practitioners have sampled and messed around with most other popular music forms, so why not country? Texas-based country "Hick Hop" artist Cowboy Troy and Lil Wayne, hip hop's rapper du jour, have set foot on CMA (Country Music Awards) stages as both presenter and performer in 2004 and 2008, respectively. And when Snoop Dogg starts doing collaborations with Willie Nelson ("My Medicine"), rhyming about weed and pimping over happening harmonicas and bodacious banjos, or appearing on Johnny Cash remixed compilations (he re-recorded Cash's 1956 classic "I Walk the Line"), you know it ain't over until the Fat Joe sings. Street corner seers, rap pundits (and hip hop book authors) might say that country and rap share similar DNA — they both tell very realistic tales rooted in the experience of the poor layperson.

Hip hop's not dead; it's just gone global. The West might no longer be where it's at. Before anyone, including anyone from New York, goes into rope-a-dope defensive mode, consider this. Twenty years ago, a marginal music form littered with rhymes focused on the underbelly of society – poverty, drugs, junkies, sex, violence, materialism, sexism – dominating the pop charts, but plastered with Parental Advisory stickers. For some adults, the apocalypse has already happened. The rap rev-

In Defense of Hipsterism

The Cool Kids, a taste-making hip hop duo from Chicago, have been called everything from the future of rap to the vanguards of hipster rap. In this 2008 interview with me, group leader Antoine "Mikey Rocks" Reed goes for broke, dispelling the myths surrounding the subgenre his group allegedly co-founded.

What exactly is Hipster Rap and did your group do anything to invent the genre?

I absolutely hate that term, man. Critics created this movement because that's human nature. People have to categorize to make it easier to understand it, so I understand why it was being done, but that don't make it right. It's just wrong. Given the connotation that comes along with the genre, it's a negative one. It suggests that somebody's doing it for the fad, the novelty of it. We've only been called that by writers who just found out about us after the fact, although we've been rocking shows for the last five years.

Some critics cite Hipster Rap scenes as being largely responsible for killing the soul of the movement, of being more wrapped up in fashion trends than the actual music itself. Do you agree?

Hip hop is not anywhere near being dead. And it's not being reborn. It's just chapter two. Hip hop is a neverending book. Chapter two is a little different from the first chapter, but it's still hip hop. People always talk about the death of the Golden Era of rap, but kids that are fourteen and fifteen years old now, this is their golden era. They don't feel the vibe that everybody was feelin' when Big Daddy Kane first came out. If you're fourteen years old, you're gonna remember Soulja Boy, Barack Obama, 9/11...there's gonna be

olution was never meant to be sanitized by bureaucrats, so it had to travel elsewhere to be re-birthed.

One of the only ways hip hop will survive is if it embraces globalization. When I interviewed Public Enemy's multiple golden eras, it just depends on where you're at, at that time.

How do you respond to criticism that rap after 2005 has become largely apolitical?

I think hip hop is beyond race and color boundaries. I don't think it will ever go back to being owned by one specific group or one specific culture or area. It's outgrown that, and it's never going back to that. It will be global, forever. Kids in Japan know how to access American music, and if they like hip hop, they gonna listen to it. They don't feel wrong for rapping a Dr. Dre song. They rap that shit front to back, they know the lyrics. And they shouldn't feel bad about that.

Your group has been called the future of rap, so what will the future of rap look like?

Well, we love sampling. It's one of the most beautiful things that music has ever seen – taking something and turning it into something completely different. Ain't nothing new under the sun man, new music is made up of all recycled materials. There's gonna be a new sound of snares, but those snares all come from the same source snare. They're (producers) just equalizing them different, making the reverb sound different. I don't see hip hop taking a techno turn, where the BPM's (beats per minute) get all higher. The foundation will always be there – nice groovy drums that you can bounce to. Cool bass lines that hit you in the heart real nice. The metaphor for rap music is like making cake. No matter what kind of cake you make, you still gonna use egg, flour and frosting. You know what I mean.

Chuck D in 1998, he sounded eerily prophetic: "To me, hip hop has never been about selling records to people twelve to eighteen years old in the eastern part of the US. It's bigger than that. Hip hop has always had Latin,

Caribbean, European and African influences, so its reach into the outer reaches of the world outside of the West, is not entirely new." Rap desperately needs to look to these elder voices for knowledge, wisdom and understanding.

The (Rap) Revolution Will Be Digitized

To prevent hip hop from becoming a dead art, left in a museum for future generations to look at alongside dinosaurs, we need only look to the World Wide Web for inspiration. We can now download and build playlists from our fave rappers from Brazil to Bangladesh on our iPods. It's where global hip hop junkies jonesing (craving) for the good stuff can always get that hit.

It's an era when the mere idea of people buying CDs or tuning into a radio or TV show to hear their favorite tunes is passé, a faded relic, thanks to Napster founder Shawn Fanning. We can swap songs — encoded in MP3 file format — across the world, over the Internet, avoiding such inconveniences as geographical boundaries, smug record-store clerks, lineups and, oh yeah, paying.[3] When some teens and twenty somethings are informed that the latest music from their rap heroes will cost $16 plus sales tax, they might ponder this for all of twenty seconds and then head straight to limewire.com and download the album in under six minutes. At no cost. Anyone can now download the entire history of music, especially if they don't think they'll get caught. And then they can brag about it on their blog and tweet you the evidence. In the immediate future we will see many going-out-of-business signs on CD stores. And major label buildings being con-

verted into lofts and condominiums. Technology —
embrace it or go bust.

Whether hip hop loses its teeth and mutates into Hip
Slop or morphs into Trip Bop (a mythical world where
trip hop meets be-bop), a few things are for certain. We
don't want rap to end up like jazz and blues, other historically black musics playing to near-empty coffee houses.
Or even worse, as fodder for VH1's *Behind the Music*.
Likewise, we pray that the Auto-Tune program — a vocal
pitch correction software that acts as an upgrade on heavily sampled renegade funkster Roger Troutman's Talkbox
— does not continue to prod rap vocalists into auto pilot-
ing their new releases. Us hip hop nationers and new-
school millennials do not want to, pardon the pun, auto
tune out of the genre. As we hip hop generationers get
older, and want to have the world take more seriously the
study and preservation of our culture, we can all feel
secure in the fact that there are more than three hundred
courses on hip hop (including one on Lil' Kim!) being
offered at colleges and universities across North America.

The Cool Kids' Mikey Rocks, as a vanguard of the
new school of hip hop, finds the mere mention of the
death of rap extremely offensive. "It's disturbing to me,
man, and upsetting that these writers and critics think
that they can take away something that's been in the
making for decades. You dictate when it's over just
because you write for this magazine? What gives you that
power? If you're not a musician, you don't have the right
to give that type of speech. Unless someone goes into all
the archives and deletes it from history, it ain't going

nowhere, it's never gonna die. Ragtime jazz still exists, there aren't as many ragtime jazz musicians but you can go get a Count Basie record from the record store down the street."[4]

The wildly popular music video game *Guitar Hero* repatriated bored, alienated youth (and their parents) to rock out like it was the 1980s all over again, when rock music reigned supreme in the US. In the same way, *Scratch: The Ultimate DJ* game, described as a "guitar hero for hip hoppers" is expected to cement the genre's status as a long-term cultural phenomenon and to convert non-rap audiences into raging closeted DJ scratch fanatics.

Rap music will always be around because it is an inherently rebellious music, even at its worst of times, with full corporate infiltration. As Chuck D said in an interview with me in 1998: "Rap is always about rebelling against something. When I came out I was rebelling against the materialism and gangsterism, which itself was a rebellion against black nationalism. When good sense gets too heavy and everybody tries to make too much sense to make a dollar, people are gonna rebel against that too."

Now there's some much-needed hip hope.

International Hip Hop Timeline

1970 Jamaican Deejay U-Roy climbs Jamaican music charts with three Top Ten songs, singing in a style called "toasting" (rhymed storytelling over a beat), creating a foundation for what would soon be called "emceeing or rapping."

1977 German band Kraftwerk releases "Trans-Europe Express," which would be the foundation for Afrika Bambaataa's Electro Funk sound and early dance floor smash "Planet Rock."

1980 The term "rapso" is invented by Calypsonian Brother Resistance to describe a distinctly Trinidadian style of street poetry that resembles a fusion of soca music with hip hop. The early lyricisms reflect the feelings of black power protest in Trinidad in the 1970s.

1982 The first international hip hop concert tour, featuring Afrika Bambaataa, Fab 5 Freddy and the Double Dutch Girls, goes to Europe, marking the start of hip hop's worldwide reach.

Malcolm McLaren, manager of seminal UK punk rock band, the Sex Pistols, releases *Buffalo Gals* 12 inch. This British appropriation of American rap takes the world by storm and becomes a major hit on both sides of the Atlantic.

1983 Japanese hip hop begins when Charlie Ahearn's *Wild Style* film is shown in Tokyo, and the Wild Style Tour, featuring the Rock Steady Crew, hits town. Street musicians start to breakdance in Yoyogi Park, and DJ Krush becomes a world-renowned DJ from the Yoyogi Park scene.

1988 Female rapper Michie Mee is the first Canadian to sign a deal with an American record label, Priority, home to stalwarts Audio Two ("Top Billin'").

1990 First international b-boy/girl Battle of the Year (originally called "The International Breakdance Cup") features performances by TDB (Germany/UK), Crazy Force Crew (Switzerland) and City Rockers (Germany).

France's MC Solaar's debut single, "*Bouge de là*" (Take a Hike), goes platinum (sales of over 100,000), and his debut album, *Qui sème le vent récolte le tempo*, sells 400,000 copies, leading to eventual collaborations with De La Soul.

1991 Ghanaian "Godfather of Hiplife" Reggie Rockstone births the Hiplife genre, a fusion of traditional highlife music and hip hop, mixed with reggae.

1993 Tommy Boy label releases *Planet Rap*, the first compilation to feature tracks from rappers around the world.

South Africa's apartheid government tries to ban rap due to its role in the struggle for the freedom of all races. Hip hop becomes a legal art practice the same year, allowing rap music on radio and television. Kwaito, a music genre that blends house music with rap and indigenous South African languages, emerges in Soweto.

1994 The first female Australian hip hop artist to receive national recognition in Australia is Opi Nelson. Her hip hop/ragamuffin rap collaboration "Last Train," with Australian Record Industry Association (ARIA) awardees Paul Kelly and Christine Anu, hits the National Top 10.

1995 UK Trip Hop, a fusion of hip hop and down-tempo electronic music, is birthed and popularized in Bristol, with the success of Massive Attack, Portishead and Tricky albums.

1998 The Arabic rap scene is popularized by DAM, a Palestinian group based in Israel, who blend Arabic melodies and hip hop beats. The content of their songs is largely focused on the many conflicts between Israel and Palestine.

1999 Korea's Drunken Tiger group forms in response to Ice Cube's "Black Korea" song, which talks about tensions between Korean shopkeepers and African Americans in Los Angeles. The group uses music as a means to promote racial harmony.

2000 Brazil's MV Bill, the country's most respected political rapper and social justice advocate, embarks on a tour of Brazil's shantytowns. A resident of the notoriously violent "City of God" favela, Bill interviews and shoots documentary footage of sixteen teenagers about their hopes and frustrations. Their stories are later collected in his book, *Pig Head*. All sixteen of those teenagers are now dead.

2001 The son of Chinese immigrants raised in Miami, Jin wins BET's 106 and Park Freestyle Friday's competition. His "Learn Chinese" hit song is the first video ever to be played on MTV Chi, a spinoff network of MTV targeted at Chinese Americans.

2002 The Cuban government forms the Cuban Rap Agency, with its own record label and magazine.

2003 Scenesters in London, England, invent Grime, a fusion of dancehall, hip hop and UK garage, recorded with high BPM and two-step break beats. Genre poster boy Dizzee Rascal's *Boy in Da Corner* wins the 2003 Mercury Music Prize.

2004 Reggaeton, a form of Latin American dance music originating in Panama, mixes hip hop, reggae and dancehall with Latin rhythms and Spanish raps. It takes off worldwide, aided by releases by Tego Calderon and Daddy Yankee.

Haitian Wyclef Jean of multi-platinum rap act the Fugees produces *Sak Pasé Presents: Welcome to Haiti Creole 101*, marking the 200th anniversary of Haiti's independence from slavery.

2005 Bollyhood Records, founded by an Australian-bred South Asian woman, Ashlene Nand, releases *BHOOD*, the first compilation of Indian-flavored hip hop and R&B, featuring exclusive collaborations between South Asian and urban American artists.

2006 The documentary film *Hiphopistan* examines the impact of hip hop culture on Turkish youth in Istanbul, providing a glimpse into how rap plays out in a predominantly Muslim society.

2008 Morocco's first-ever national hip hop music and breakdance competition is won by female rappers Flow Tigresses and female breakdance troupe Anti Boys Crew.

New Zealand-based, Samoan emcee Savage sells over one million downloads of his hit single "Swing," helped in part by its placement in hit US movie *Knocked Up*.

2009 Bakhtawar Bhutto, daughter of assassinated Pakistani former prime minister Benazir Bhutto, releases rap tribute "I Would Take the Pain Away."

Notes

1 The Audacity of Hip Hop

1. Jeff Johnson, BET anchor interview with Barack Obama on hip hop culture, YouTube, www.youtube.com, February 2008.
2. Keith Caulfield, ed., "Jay-Z Scores 10th No. 1 Album On the *Billboard* 200," Billboard.biz, November 14, 2007.
3. Stephen M. Silverman, "50 Cent Selling 53 Room Connecticut Mansion," *People*, May 3, 2007.
4. For a great piece on the political context of rap's development see Clarence Lusane, "Rap, Race and Politics," *Race and Class* 35, 1 (1993), 43.

2 The Old School and the Elements

1. Jeff Chang, *Can't Stop Won't Stop* (New York: St. Martin's Press, 2005), 13.
2. Raquel Z. Rivera, *New York Ricans from the Hip Hop Zone* (New York: Palgrave Macmillan, 2003).
3. David Toop, *Rap Attack* (London: Serpent's Tail, 1984), 31-32.
4. Cheo Hodari Coker, *The Life, Death and Afterlife of the Notorious B.I.G.* (New York: Three Rivers Press, 2003), 20.
5. Wayne Marshall, "Hearing Hip Hop's Jamaican Accent," *Institute for Studies in American Music*, Spring 2005.
6. Ibid.
7. Joey Garfield, director, *Breath Control: History of the Human Beat Box*, 2002.
8. See results at www.battleoftheyear.de/past-events.html.
9. Mr Wiggles, one of the original b-boys, breaks it down at www.mrwiggles.biz/hip_hop_influences.htm.
10. The Hip Hop Chess Federation, which mixes music, martial arts and chess, has done some great research linking the traditions. See www.hiphopchessfederation.org/.
11. Ibid.
12. For more information on this innovation, check out www.johncage.info/workscage/landscape1.html. This composition can be downloaded from many sources on the Web.

13. Sacha Jenkins et al., *Ego Trip's Book of Rap Lists* (New York: St. Martin's Press, 1999), 271.

14. Todd S. Inoue, "Beats Generation," *Metro Active*, November 7, 1996.

15. *Tales of the Turntable: Filipino American DJs of the Bay Area*, art exhibit by Melanie Cagonot, San Mateo County History Museum, Redwood City, California, February 2002.

16. Victor Hugo Viesca, "With Style: Filipino Americans and the Making of American Urban Culture," essay delivered at 9th Filipino Biennial, Los Angeles, July 27, 2002.

17. Ibid.

18. *Tales of the Turntable*, art exhibit by Melanie Cagonot.

19. Renee Graham, "Will Ruling on Samples Chill Rap," *Boston Globe*, September 14, 2004.

20. All references to dollars are in US currency.

3 What's Race Got to Do with It?

1. I covered the inaugural event for *Now* magazine. See the National Hip Hop Political Convention website, www.nhhpc.org.

2. Greg Tate, ed., *Everything But the Burden: What White People Are Taking from Black Culture* (New York: Harlem Moon/Broadway Books, 2003). The book has several great essays on the appropriation and ultimate takeover of black music.

3. "White People Should Make White Music," Yahoo.com, September 27, 2005.

4. I've interviewed Upski a number of times, for the *Source* and *Now* magazine, and brought him to Toronto to speak on rap and race.

5. Bakari Kitwana, *Why White Kids Love Hip Hop* (New York: Basic Civitas, 2005), 82-92.

6. In 2006 New York State banned the use of the word, though it was never clear how they could enforce the ban.

7. Hillary Crosley, "Nas Select N Word for New Album Title," Billboard.com, October 15, 2007.

8. The NAACP held a symbolic funeral for the N-word in the streets of Detroit on July 9, 2007.

9. For statistics on HIV/AIDS in South Africa see www.avert.org/safricastats.htm.

10. I conducted this interview with Tumi in the midst of his summer 2008 tour.
11. Statistics Canada, Census 2006, Canada's Aboriginal Population, www.statcan.gc.ca/pub/11-008-x/2009001/article/10864-eng.htm.
12. In June 2008 the Canadian federal government offered an official apology for the harmful residential school legacy. Yet apologies about past wrongs are meaningless if the First Nations community is being neglected today.
13. Chantle Beeso, HipHopCanada.com interview with Team Rez Official, July 11, 2008.
14. Brett Cyr, "Hip Hop Hits the Rez," Aboriginal Youth Network News, September 7, 2004.
15. Chantle Beeso, HipHopCanada.com interview.
16. Andrew Mayeda, "Bush Greets PM: Yo," *National Post*/Canwest News Service, July 7, 2008.
17. Minya Oh, "Bling Bling Added to Oxford Dictionary," MTV.com News, April 30, 2003.
18. Ibid.
19. James Montgomery, "Crunk Really Ain't Dead: Word Makes It into Merriam-Webster Dictionary," MTV.com News, July 12, 2007.

4 Hip Hop's Economic Stimulus Plan

1. *Forbes* has produced an annual list of the richest rappers since 2006.
2. Check out www.simmonslathan.com.
3. Stephen Silverman, "P. Diddy Wins Fashion Industry Top Award," *People*, June 8, 2004.
4. Naomi Klein, *No Logo* (Toronto: Random House, 2000), 84.
5. Mark Anthony Neal and Murray Forman, *That's the Joint: The Hip-Hop Studies Reader* (New York: Routledge, 2004), 164.
6. Melody Weinstein, *Remixed in Japan* (New York: Melo Films, 2007).
7. Xuexin Liu, "The Hip Hop Impact on Japanese Youth Culture," *Southeast Review of Asian Studies* XXVII (2005).

5 Hip Hop Herstory and Pride Rap

1. Atlanta's Spellman University led a boycott of Nelly and his music in 2005 for his depiction of women in his videos.

2. Imane Belhaj, "Female Rappers Win Morocco's First National Hip Hop Competition," Magharebia.com, May 12, 2008.

3. AllHipHop.com, November 11, 2008.

4. Sujatha Fernandes, *Cuba Represent!: Cuban Arts, State Power, and the Making of New Revolutionary Cultures* (Durham, NC: Duke University Press, 2006), 109-117.

5. "Kanye West," *Entertainment Weekly*, October 2007.

6 Rap's Social Conscience

1. The MySpace page for the Stop the Violence Movement features links to the "Self Destruction" song and video featuring a who's who of East Coast rap talents weighing in on violence.

2. In a May 1971 *Playboy* magazine interview by Hugh Hefner, John Wayne says, "I believe in White Supremacy."

3. Billy Johnson Jr., "The Coup's Album Cover Meant to Symbolize Group's Anti-Establishment Stance," Yahoo Music News, http://new.music.yahoo.com, September 14, 2001.

4. See www.myspace.com/rbgfamily for a description of the political programs that Dead Prez and affiliates are involved in.

5. Bakari Kitwana, "The Cotton Club," *Village Voice*, June 21, 2005.

6. Faiza Saleh Ambah, "Saudi Hip Hop's Painful Birth," msnbc.com, May 2, 2008.

7. CIA World Factbook, www.cia.gov/library/publications/ the-world-factbook. (Numbers include blacks and mulattos.)

8. Marc Lacey, "Cuba's Rap Vanguard Reaches Beyond the Party Line," *New York Times*, December 15, 2006.

9. I interviewed two Cuban rappers about the relationship between the state and hip hop and they chose to remain anonymous on this point for political reasons.

10. Rand Corporation, "Exposure to Degrading Versus Non-Degrading Music Lyrics and Sexual Behaviour Among Youth," www.rand.org, 2006.

11. Shereen El Feki, "Banlieue Blues," *Prospect*, May 2007, 134.

12. NPR (National Public Radio) Report, December 14, 2005.

13. Dominique Vidalon, "French President's Son Outed as Hip Hop Producer," Reuters News Agency, January 14, 2008.

7 The Globalization of Hip Hop

1. Adrienne Mong, NBC News, August 19, 2008.
2. Plug in Sara and Ryusei on YouTube, www.youtube.com. These clips must be seen to be believed!
3. Sanjay Sharma, John Hutnyk and Ashwani Sharma, eds., *Disorienting Rhythms: The Politics of the New Asian Dance Music* (London: Zed Books, 1996), 32-37.
4. Joe D'Angelo, "Dr. Dre, Interscope Stung with 500 Million Lawsuit Over Addictive," MTV News, September 19, 2002.
5. Amy Eisinger, "Snoop Dogg Goes Bollywood with Singh Is King," *New York Times*, August 6, 2008.
6. "Militant Senegalese Rapper Didier Awadi," *Guardian*, February 15, 2008.
7. All K'naan quotes are from an interview I conducted with him in 2004. I produced his artist biography for Sony/BMG before the fame and glory and presented his breakout concert in Toronto in 2005. Although I've presented hundreds of concerts since, it remains one of my favorite hip hop moments.
8. See Song Meanings at www.songmeanings.net/lyric.php?lid= 3530822107858656930.
9. From my interview with K'naan in 2004.

8 Black to the Future

1. Lil Wayne's "Lollipop" went to #1 on the *Billboard* Top 100 Charts in May 2008.
2. "Tupac Shakur's Posthumous CD Loyal to the Game Debuts at No. 1," *Jet*, January 17, 2005.
3. Spencer E Ante, "The E-Biz 25: Shawn Fanning," *Business Week*, May 15, 2000.
4. This quote is from an interview I conducted with the Cool Kids on December 5, 2008, just before they played their opening set on the Bounce 2K Tour with Q-Tip.

For Further Information

Essential Reading

Chang, Jeff. *Can't Stop, Won't Stop: A History of the Hip-Hop Generation*. New York: St. Martin's Press, 2005.

Durand, Alain-Phillipe. *Black, Blanc, Beur: Rap Music and Hip-Hop Culture in the Francophone World*. Maryland: Scarecrow Press, 2003.

Gondry, Ian. *Hip-Hop Japan: Rap and the Path of Cultural Globalization*. North Carolina: Duke University Press, 2006.

Kitwana, Bakari. *The Hip Hop Generation: Young Blacks and the Crisis in African American Culture*. New York: Basic Civitas Books, 2003.

Morgan, Joan. *When Chickenheads Come Home to Roost: A Hip-Hop Feminist Breaks It Down*. New York: Simon and Schuster, 2000.

Rose, Tricia. *Black Noise*. New Hampshire: Wesleyan University Press, 1994.

Wimsatt, William "Upski." *Bomb the Suburbs*. Chicago: Subway and Elevated Press Company, 1994.

Essential Viewing

Ahearn, Charlie. *Wild Style*. 1982.

Ahearn, Charlie and Tony Silver. *Style Wars*. 1983.

Bravo, Vee. *Estilo Hip-Hop*. 2009.

Chalfant, Henry. *From Mambo to Hip Hop*. 2006.

Herson, Ben and Magee McIlvane. *Democracy in Dakar*. 2007.

Lee, Benson. *Planet B-Boy*. 2007.

Offer, Erin. *Counting Headz: South Afrika's Sistaz in Hip Hop*. 2006.

Raimist, Rachel. *Nobody Knows My Name*. 1999.

Reis, Jon. *Bomb It*. 2008.

Weinstein, Melody. *Remixed in Japan*. 2006.

Zimbalist, Jeff. *Favela Rising*. 2005.

Acknowledgments

To the island of Jamaica for imbuing in me the Maroon, Rastafarian and ancestral spirits needed to endure Babylon. To the Most High.

To my mom, Pearlita Ellis, for instilling in me the love of words and power of hard work. Pops Josiah for providing for me, being the coolest cat on the planet, and for blasting them loud reggae riddims into me from the womb. Night nurse. To my brother, Milton, who has always had my back through thick and thin and taught me many things about how to be a man. Who doesn't know Milton the Mayor?

To my other half and wifey, Karen Bell, who is hands down my best friend, and the greatest mom there is (but I'm biased). A true lioness. A rare breed of woman.

To my seedlings and reasons for being, Solomon "Pretty Boy" Bell-Higgins and Shiloh Bell-Higgins. May you both take the Bell and Higgins family traditions and make waves, make change, make headlines, travel the (hip hop) world, invest in real estate.

The Groundwood Books crew — Patsy Aldana for not only being the sharpest publisher I've met, and I've met aplenty, but because she gets "it." Jane Springer for helping to turn my musings, rants and recollections into words that will breathe life into many youth around the globe.

Editor/broadcaster Zuhair Kashmeri for understanding that without opportunity, smarts can never be nurtured. Ellie Kirzner for being a good darn editor. Nicholas Davis for being a friend, mentor, and crucial sounding board for me, for like, forever. Samson Okalow, where you at? Clifton Joseph is the Man (and the Reverend Swami). Paulene and Dameion, mi haffi big yu up, and Big It Up.

Librarian/author Ken Setterington for his foresight and insight.

Comedian Dave Chappelle, cartoonist Aaron McGruder and Afro-futurist Greg Tate, whose respective worldviews eerily influence my own.

To authors/educators George Elliott Clarke, Althea Prince, Zanana Akande and Rinaldo Walcott for being unrepentantly brilliant in the face of…

To the new school (you all better look out for the work from these uber talented not-so young 'uns I call my friends): Emily Mills, Brandi Costain, Ian "Kamau," Brandon Hay, Ras King, Che Kothari, Marwan

Lucas, Mark Campbell, Souljah Rose, Jason Richards, Jelani "J-Wyze," Raoul Juneja, Dave Guenette, Jules Bedeau, Salima Rawji, Julia Che, Mindbender, Akilah Child, Theology 3 and Alexis Johnson for teaching me that learning goes both ways. These are a few of the younger hip hop generationers that directly inspire me. Saada Branker, AfriKaren/Tuku/Harlow, Alicia Dyson, Respect.

To P-Frank Williams (The Source, thank you), Elizabeth Mendez Berry (the world ain't ready, but Armand is), Upski (the world is ready, finally).

Support the black press. *Share, Pride, Word Magazine, Sway* and the like.

To my industry peeps, supporters and foundation hombres, Ivan Evidente, Fiona Bloom, Jody Laraya, Heller Rosen, Will Strickland, Sol Guy, Greg "Gee Wunder" Baptiste, Jay Devonish, Dave "Click" Cox, Golden Chile, Theology 3, Charles/Bernard Lewis, Junior (Monica's), Maurice Davis, Ivla Pollard, Ricky "Lindon" Black, Marlee Ave., K-4CE, Michee Mee, The Good Doctor Kenneth Montague, Owen "OG" Gordon, Kwame Younge, Norman "Otis" Richmond, Adrian Eccleston, Sandra Whiting, Billy "The Mad Blogger" Bryans, Mayday and Di Hoffishall Harrow, Matte Babel, Adrian Eccleston, Carl Cassell, Dennis Passley, Alok Sharma and Zenia, Master T & Roxy Paula, Alton Morgan, Fennella Bruce, Dwight Ireland, Dwight Drummond, Ashante Infantry, Amy Katz, Webley! (aka Diana), Jay Cohen, A Man Called Ramos, Ian Peters, Tabby Johnson, Peculiar I, Shaka, Steve Carty/Tersia/Aya, Ryan Bailey, Isaiah Trickey.

Richard "Fresh" Mitchell, C-Wizdom, through thick and thin, the struggle continues.

DJ Andy Williams for providing the soundtrack. And DJ L'Oqenz too.

I am righteous but ruthless, like King Sun. And when the world zigs, I zag.

Index